What others have said about The Children Left Behind

"In her book, many of Jill's students tell their own stories as her educational memoir unfolds. These poignant stories will capture the readers' minds and hearts and help them to understand why we must make important changes in our educational institutions. *The Children Left Behind* is a must-read for parents, teachers, administrators, legislators, and anyone who cares about our future generations. Jill's passion to educate our children emotionally as well as academically is contagious."

—Joyce Stanley

Retired School Teacher, Abingdon, VA

I0086969

"Jill has emphasized through personal experiences the tremendous need for increased focus on improving emotional skills of students..... having worked thirty-four years with young people in public education, I must agree!"

—Wayne C. Bastian, Ed.D.

Retired Teacher, High School Principal, and School District Superintendent

"I am Lindy in the book. My story is a success because Jill helped make my world safe. I am grateful to her and others who understand the issues that children bring to school. I wouldn't be where I am today.... living life to the fullest, married and two children....without the emotional support I received as a child."

—Lindy

Wife and Mother

The Children Left Behind

The Children Left Behind

The Children Left Behind

Jill Lemons Doty, M.S. Ed.

The Forgotten Education

http://www.theforgotteneducation.com

Acknowledgements

As this book project is completed there are many people I want to thank for their significant contributions. Each part of this project has special meaning. The cover of the book is a picture I took a few years ago at Fort Robinson State Park in Nebraska. I was fortunate to have grown up with both sets of grandparents living nearby in Crawford, and consequently have many memories where this picture was taken. I will always be thankful to my parents for giving me the "gift" of a childhood.

One of my colleagues, Becky Miller, fixed technical computer issues, formatted the book for publishing, and most importantly designed the book cover and logo for **The Forgotten Education** website. Thank you Becky for your expertise and patience as we created these important visual images which will serve to illustrate the messages I am hoping to convey.

To Wendy Thompson, another colleague and photographer, thank you for so graciously working to get my picture for the book and website.

During the summer of 2012, as I diligently worked to complete the majority of the writing for this book, I was fortunate to have met Brandi Johnson in a metalsmithing class. As we sat making jewelry and visiting it seemed we were destined to have met that summer. Brandi graduated from the high school where I have been employed since moving to Colorado. She offered her expertise, skills, and talents in developing the website and consulting during the writing of the book. Brandi, you donated so many hours to this project. I cannot begin to thank you enough. It has been a joy to not only work with you but to also get to know you as we've shared many of our life experiences along the way.

The past decade has been full of changes in my life. Moving from Virginia to Colorado was certainly one of the most momentous events. Through a dear friend in Virginia I was fortunate to meet Gayle Stringer, editor of this book. We have many unique bonds beginning with the fact that she and I have both lived in Fort Collins, Colorado and Abingdon, Virginia! We share a love for each of these places. Gayle, I value you as a "master teacher," talented artist, dear friend, and now as my editor. You gave up hours that turned into weeks working on this manuscript. I am so grateful to have been able to share this long, arduous task with such a good friend. You joined me in my passion and pursuit to share the important messages I have written about. I could not have done this without you!

To my dear family and close friends, thank you for always being there for me.

And finally to my cherished children,
Katie and Drew, I love you both with all my heart.

Author's Note

The stories I have written about come from my years of working in education. The events in this memoir are described according to my perception and understanding of the events. The names, places, and some details have been altered to protect the privacy and anonymity of the students and co-workers to whom they refer.

Contents

- 1 -
The Silence Ends

Many factors have kept this manuscript from completion. There have been time constraints, insecurities, and a move halfway across the country. But most of all, there has been the fear that telling the stories may compromise the privacy of my students.

Yet it is their stories, representing children across our nation, that provide the significance, value, and meaning to the messages within this book.

"And the day came when the risk to remain tight in a bud was more painful than the risk it took to bloom."

-Anais Nin

My intentions are to reveal the daily realities of education along with reflections, ideas, and hope for inspiring new, constructive changes.

I have kept their voices silent long enough. They reveal the dire need for meaningful educational reforms that would facilitate fundamental improvements in the peace and happiness of our children, families, schools, and communities.

Their voices offer insight and understanding regarding the plight of the American Educational System. The following statements embody my devoted pursuit to complete this writing project, and my passion for the necessity of teaching emotional intelligence—**the forgotten education**.

The following are actual words spoken by children and parents. They represent the things none of us want to know, but must know. They represent their lives, and why, on any given day, learning can be a challenge:

"I counted every time my mom would hit her. She would scream and I would count. I ran in on number fourteen and yelled at her to stop."

"In my perfect day, I would have a house with a white fence and I would come down the stairs and my mom would be fixing me breakfast."

"I feel sad and bad every day."

"I need to ask you some questions about devorse[sic].
Please contact me in Mrs. Anderson's room."

"I wish he wouldn't drink so much."

"I had to sit on the rug in her room all day. I could only get up to go to the bathroom. She says I'm grounded until February."

"I'm jealous because other kids have their moms and I don't."

"I got this reputation in my other schools. I just
want a clean start....I want my dad."

"I'm not doing so good in my grades. Please help me."

"What do I put down on the sheet if my brother died?"

"He's gonna be mad at me, but you all need to know what he's
been through. I was abused as a child and used to wear long
sleeve shirts all the time to cover the bruises, but that is nothing compared to my son. He has seen more in his life than
any of us. He was sexually abused and then sat this far away
from his step dad and watched him blow his head off."

"My mom needs counseling. She has part of my step dad and his
glasses with blood on them....we had to clean it up afterwards."

"I would have rather taken a beating than go to
school. The day I turned sixteen, I quit school."

"We got run out of North Carolina. About ten guys came to our
house and told my dad they would get him so we had to leave. I've
been in North Carolina, then Florida, then Tennessee, and now

here. They were teaching North Carolina history when I was there, and here they are teaching Virginia history....it's confusing."

"I hurt so badly. Why is the alcohol more important than I am? My head understands, but still my heart breaks."

"My grandpa was the only one who understood me, and now he is gone, and it is like my whole family is falling apart. I loved my grandpa, and I miss him."

The impetus for writing this book came shortly after The No Child Left Behind Act was passed over a decade ago. My previous years spent teaching had already left me full of frustrations about our educational system. Once the realities of the legislation became apparent, my frustrations grew even greater.

Although many eloquent authors have written before me about issues related to teaching and learning, their words have gone unheard by those empowered to legislate reforms. What was lacking in education was not addressed in the No Child Left Behind Act. Instead, illogical, cumbersome changes were mandated.

Each passing year becomes more difficult than the one before as these changes have been implemented. The voices of the children echo louder and more often with no signs of reprieve in sight. Instead, we are faced with the major hallmark of reform: "testing" for accountability—testing and testing so we can collect mountains of data to evaluate students, teachers, administrators, and entire school systems. It is wrong and further does nothing to fill the voids of **the forgotten education**.

What is **the forgotten education**? It is the teaching of social/emotional skills curriculum aimed at increasing emotional intelligence. Daniel Goleman, author of the book, *Emotional Intelligence*, defines it as "a person's ability to be aware of, and to control, his own emotions. It involves the development of self-restraint and compassion in dealing with others, the ability to motivate oneself and to work with passion and persistence."

Forgotten in education are standards addressing the affective domain which encompasses motivation, attitudes, stereotypes, perceptions, and feelings. This domain is extremely significant to cognitive functioning, yet widely ignored.

Even though every human being needs skill development in this area, it is not required curriculum. Ironically, I recently read an article that stated only two percent of the population will need algebra skills, yet most students are forced to take several years of algebra to meet a one-size-fits-all set of graduation requirements.

> "Blatant and harmful misappropriations of standardized tests for fallacious uses have been a constant of America's historical experience with standardized testing in schools...tests intended to evaluate individual achievement have been used to base unfounded conclusions of the educational quality of entire school systems."
>
> -Peter Sacks, *Standardized Minds*

- 2 -
The Fallout

Rigid standards and protocols for teachers and testing for accountability come with inherent issues. As priorities have shifted, instead of improvements, we have lost much of what was good in education with more children left behind than ever before. It is important to also acknowledge the excellent teachers lost along the way—teachers who had their knowledge of best practices stripped from them as they were forced to teach to tests to be certain the data reflected student mastery of government-driven standards. This has become the primary measure of accountability.

> "Standardized tests reward passive, superficial learning, drive instruction in undesirable directions, and thwart meaningful educational reform."
>
> -Peter Sacks, Standardized Minds

Everyone wants accountability, but when students' scores are used to determine a teacher's effectiveness, it is most detrimental to the students. In this book, you will read about students who most likely would not meet state standards and therefore, often become the "unwanted" in the classroom. Ironically, the whole point of No Child Left Behind is rendered moot.

Conscientious teachers have always toiled to reach all students. As in any profession, not all are conscientious. The problem with evaluating teachers on student growth is that it unfairly punishes those who are. These teachers are often already overloaded with the "unwanted" students because they are the most effective in working with them. Administrators under the same evaluation stress, feel inclined to give these teachers even more "unwanted" students. The conscientious teacher is, by nature, a target for exhaustion and burn out due to their unwavering, valiant work ethics.

No Child Left Behind was an honorable goal. Unfortunately, it creates the opposite effect; the "unwanted" have become liabilities to their educational institutions.

Years ago when I was teaching, I welcomed the students no one else wanted into my classroom and embraced the challenge of reaching them. Forging this path required time, creativity, and patience. In today's world, I would not be afforded this flexibility and further would have the added stress associated with trying to fit all students into the same mold.

Later in my career while working as a school counselor in Virginia, I was required to attend a training meeting. A power point presentation "told the story" of inflexible, unrealistic government control. The program had been created by a State committee and was used to train teachers on "pacing guides." Pacing guides were timelines for teaching the state standards of learning. The significant point of this training was to be certain teachers understood exactly what they were to teach and when. Further, it was made clear that everyone was expected to utilize their pacing guides. One slide contained the phrase, "Pacing guides or die." To those of us in the training, this was not humorous. I left feeling frustrated and concerned. How had our schools come to this point of extreme and inappropriate government control?

As a beginning teacher, my decision to leave the first grade reader for a few weeks to use a set of "monster-themed" books written by children would not have been allowed in standards-driven Virginia. Incorporating math measurement concepts by baking a giant monster cookie to culminate the reading unit would also not be allowed. Activities such as these did not exist in the "pacing guides."

My lessons were not careless attempts to avoid learning objectives, but instead a conscious choice to take a different route, with the hope of finding motivation for learning along the way. Many teaching materials were stifling and boring. Providing diverse methods which made learning interesting and fun would have been difficult if the expectation had been to "stay in the box and only color in the lines!"

What has happened to our freedom of "choice?" I distinctly remember from my American History class that our country was founded on the right to "choose." Why then, do we not have the choice to develop schools with differing philosophies? While I don't support the current educational reforms, others may want "test driven" accountability, and they deserve to have that choice. But, conversely, we should have the right to choose other alternatives in public education without having to form charter schools.

The Fallout

- 3 -
The Problems With Testing

When I was in graduate school taking my assessment course, the number one rule was to NEVER use assessments as the sole piece of the puzzle. Yet that premise is often ignored. Some colleges and universities understand this and are incorporating more than just the student's GPA and test scores for their admission process. They are looking for leadership, extracurricular activities, volunteer and community service, and most of all, evidence of a student's resiliency because the resilient student reflects strong emotional intelligence.

> "If the purpose for learning is to score well on a test, we've lost sight of the real reason for learning."
>
> –Jeannie Fulbright

It is also important to understand the impact created when so much emphasis is placed on academic test results. If the agreed-upon goal of education is to prepare our children to be productive members of society, we must be certain about what data would actually measure and reflect this goal. Few would disagree that we need to improve our educational system by looking for ways to help those who slip through the system unprepared; however, we should not jeopardize the opportunity schools have to foster a "love of learning" in the quest for accountability. The "love of learning" is lost when the focal point of education is passing test scores.

Emphasis on test scores as the foremost measure of school improvement forces schools into a practice of focusing on student weaknesses instead of strengths. Students become disenfranchised and overwhelmed with failure. Absent is the emphasis on their strengths. Most will never even discover them, left with only the condemning red check marks etched into their minds. These are sad educational fatalities, and yet they happen every day. The previously mentioned quote, from a parent of one of my students, reflects this reality:

"I would have rather taken a beating than go to school.
The day I turned sixteen, I quit school."

I am absolutely in support of moving past mediocrity in our schools along with improving accountability, but standardized learning and assessments only ensures mediocrity. It frustrates me to think of the enormous amounts of time, energy, and money wasted on testing which simply reflect the regurgitation of facts that are soon forgotten. With the amount of standards constantly increasing, time constraints steal opportunities teachers have for the necessary activities needed to attach meaning and relevance to the objectives.

I recall a comment I once heard in a workshop regarding the continual practice of adding new curriculum and never taking any away. The comment brought an immediate round of rousing applause from the educators in the audience. It is time to move away from the notion that increasing the volume equates to school improvement.

Instead, opportunities to foster creativity and in-depth thinking are required. Students need critical thinking skills to solve the problems they will face in their lives. Critical thinking, creativity, and one's ability to manage emotions are much harder concepts to measure and require far more time than memorization.

Doing more of what is already ineffective by extending the school day is not the answer. Yet this is occurring as pilot schools across the country lengthen their school years. Reducing and re-prioritizing standards would create the necessary time needed for more in-depth learning.

Another problem with the tests we currently utilize in education is that few people, even educators, have the necessary training to accurately interpret the scores and reach appropriate conclusions. Dr. Jane Healy, author of *Endangered Minds*, wrote about this

> "Reading furnishes the mind only with materials of knowledge; it is thinking that makes what we read ours."
>
> —John Locke

subject. The following excerpts from her book underscore some of the problems with standardized education and testing:

25

Why test scores should be taken with a grain of salt

(Taken from *Endangered Minds* by Dr. Jane Healy)

* *"Tests which show younger children's scores are rising may be focusing on the lower-level skills of word recognition and neglecting the real heart of the matter, how well they understand what they have read. Can they reason—and talk, and write—about it?*

* *When testing children on reading skills, it is relatively easy to check out phonics and other word-reading abilities. It takes much longer to find out how well students have understood a passage. Most standardized tests used today are given to large groups of children and are scored by machines. They are poor vehicles for assessing comprehension because the student is not required to formulate anything, merely fill in the bubbles, to check off one of a given set of answers.*

* *The Carnegie Council on Adolescent Development suggested that test scores do not reveal the total extent of the problem, as they are poor measures of the type of thinking abilities today's youth will need on the job.*

* *International Assessments comparing math and science performance of thirteen-year-old students from twelve countries found United States at 'rock bottom' particularly in understanding of concepts and more complex interpretation of data."*

Time has become an enormous obstacle in education. No one feels they have adequate time to accomplish all that is required of them. Constantly looming in everyone's minds are the test scores, certainly not the "love of learning."

- 4 -
No Time to Play
Forgotten Learning Domains

I will always remember my son Drew, and my oldest niece Olivia, starting kindergarten in Virginia and talking about the SOLs (Standards of Learning), most of which were completely inappropriate for kindergarten students. I was discouraged about the increased academic content in the kindergarten curriculum and the loss of "play" which resulted from these changes. The foundation of emotional intelligence begins with "play."

> "Play is the highest form of research."
>
> -Albert Einstein

I had done research on the push for early academics when starting a preschool in my local church before Drew was born. There was plenty of information about the burn-out of children who were taught to read and master other skills at early ages. Further, the subsequent negative, long-term consequences to children who are not taught the developmental skills associated with socialization was clear.

I have always been passionate about the messages in David Elkind's book, *The Hurried Child*. Written in the eighties, he described the future we now live in, and he predicted accurately writing, "When school is looked upon as an assembly line and when there is pressure to increase production, there is a temptation not only to fill the bottles faster but also to fill them earlier. Why not put in as much at kindergarten as at first grade? Why not teach fourth grade math at grade two.....Schools and school personnel are currently under pressure to produce improved test scores of pupils. We have seen that when people are under stress they become egocentric and do not-cannot-appreciate other people's needs or interests. Hence the new 'measurement-driven programs' ignore what we know about children for the same reason that parent schedules hurry children – the adults who are involved cannot put to use their knowledge about children and education. If we take some of the pressure off schools and school administrators, we will take some of the pressure off children."

His statement, "…when people are under stress they become egocentric….and cannot appreciate other people's needs or interests," is significant in understanding the importance of the learning environment. Skyrocketing stress levels in both students and adults make it a daunting task for everyone to feel and show concern for each other. Yet this is essential in learning environments.

In the video, *Emotion: Gatekeeper to Performance*, Candace Pert, Researcher at Georgetown University, along with renowned educator Susan Kovalik and physiologist, Carla Hannaford, provide interesting insights into educational systems. They describe the success of systems where students are not pushed into early academics and "hurried" as Elkind described in his book. They also review the critical role of emotions in learning, stress as an inhibiting factor, and the importance of the environment to student achievement.

> "People don't care how much you know, until they know how much you care."
>
> —John C. Maxwell

Hannaford discusses Copenhagen, Denmark, considered one of the top educational systems in the world, "based upon the amount of profound scientific research and artwork that is produced per capita," with a literacy rate of 100% in two languages. Hannaford explains that these rates include the reading of the classics.

In Copenhagen, students do not start reading instruction before the age of eight. Additionally, no tests are given until students are fourteen, and then tests are used solely to identify strengths and weaknesses. Grades are not used to compare and rank students. Students are encouraged throughout their school years. This creates calm, nurturing environments where students' creativity and learning can blossom.

In contrast, our educational system continually renames old practices concentrating on students' weaknesses in order to improve student test scores. Interventions focus on the cognitive domain typically involving extra time and tutoring assistance. The other two domains, psychomotor and affective, are rarely, if ever, considered as they relate to academic performance.

School improvement must include comprehensive approaches which encompass best practices from both the past and present. Long ago,

Benjamin Bloom outlined the three interconnected domains important in learning: the affective, the psychomotor, and the cognitive—in other words, mind, body, and spirit. You cannot separate the domains. The head (cognitive) does not become detached from the body to come to school and learn teaching objectives; it comes attached to a body (psychomotor) and a spirit (emotions) working in integral ways in all functions of life, especially in learning.

> "...children confronted with the task of learning to read before they have the requisite mental abilities can develop long-term learning difficulties."
>
> -David Elkind, The Hurried Child

Interesting to note, most educators only learn about the levels of thinking associated with the cognitive domain, never having been exposed to Bloom's work and beliefs about the learning environment and the need for appropriate student assessments. He believed that assessments should be used to help students achieve their goals versus comparing them to other students. He also was an advocate for individual differences and believed not all students should be expected to attain the same goals at the same time.

Most educator training programs also expose students to Abraham Maslow's theory of human motivation. He highlighted the importance of physical and emotional needs as essential steps to self actualization. Teachers understand that their students first need to be clothed, fed, and feel safe to learn; nevertheless, in our country, standards for students are the same, regardless of whether they come to school with their basic human needs met.

Educating the "whole child" is reflected in Susan Kovalik's ITI (Integrated Thematic Instruction) approach. Her Program combines the long-standing wisdom of Bloom and Maslow, coupled with current neuroscience research. She is a strong voice regarding the importance of the learning environment. In the video, *Emotion: Gatekeeper* to Performance, she states, **"The emotional environment is as important as the academic content itself."**

Addressing the importance of the psychomotor domain, Carla Hannaford outlined the biological explanations of how movement helps the brain function more effectively in both her book *Smart Moves*, and the above-mentioned video. She explains the biological reasons why movement is essential to all learning and further discusses that it is "absurd to learn sitting all day." If we fully understood the value of movement in improving the negative emotions, which hinder learning, we would regularly utilize movement as an academic intervention!

The title of this video needs to capture the attention of everyone associated with education reform, and serve as a slogan for school improvement because it is true: **emotion is the gatekeeper to performance!**

"The fact is that given the challenges we face, education doesn't need to be reformed—it needs to be transformed. The key to this transformation is not to standardize education, but to personalize it, to build achievement on discovering the individual talents of each child, to put students in an environment where they want to learn and where they can naturally discover their true passions."

-Ken Robinson,
The Element: How Finding Your Passion Changes Everything

- 5 -

All I Needed to Know I Learned...
In The Beginning

I graduated from college in 1982. During my first years working in elementary schools in Nebraska, I remember looking over every subject I was responsible to teach. There were so many objectives in so many subjects that were to be mastered. I felt that even if we were in school twenty-four hours a day, seven days a week, we still would not have enough time to accomplish everything.

> "We should not just teach the three R's.....instead the seven R's, Reading, writing, arithmetic, rights, responsibilities, respect, and reality."
>
> -Wayne C. Bastian, Ed.D

There were, of course, the three R's: reading, writing, and arithmetic. Then we also had social studies, grammar, science, spelling, handwriting, and art. The only breaks given to teachers were thirty minutes of physical education or music twice a week.

There was very little planning time, yet numerous subjects to plan, teach, grade, remediate, and enrich.

Now I work in a high school and I am amused when teachers fuss about too many preps. I believe an elementary teacher can easily move up to higher grades, but moving a high school teacher to the elementary level would be another story!

In that first frightful year, I also had "Pride" curriculum to teach which consisted of a four-inch thick binder full of objectives and lessons. What in the world was this "Pride" curriculum about? As I looked at the lessons, I realized this curriculum would address the social/emotional child.

After much contemplation, I decided that if perhaps I started with these materials and taught the students to get along with each other, the rest would fall into place. It seemed to me that the most efficient way to teach would be to eliminate behavioral interruptions. This would also create a more positive and relaxed environment. With that small piece of a plan, I started my first, overwhelming year of teaching.

I held a class meeting the first day and talked with the students about how we wanted our room to function and asked for their input in forming our classroom rules. I recorded their ideas on a large piece of chart paper. Examining the filled page, I told them I couldn't remember that many rules. They agreed, and we decided upon three to four basic rules that covered all the items on our chart.

Then we discussed what the consequences should be if a student broke a rule. They wanted a warning first and then time out. The time out chair was behind our cubby shelf so there wasn't anything entertaining to watch with the hope that students would want to quickly rejoin the class.

With a very at risk population of children with stories you will later read about, we forged a way to get along and learn as much as we could in all the other subjects.

Throughout all the years I've been in education, I have heard from countless employers the need for schools to teach students how to work together so they are later prepared for employment with those essential skills. Clearly midst all the academic content, **the forgotten education** is a critical element to success in the workplace.

- 6 -
The Importance of Emotional Intelligence

In his book *Emotional Intelligence*, Daniel Goleman wrote: "Educators, long disturbed by school children's lagging scores in math and reading, are realizing there is a different and more alarming deficiency: emotional illiteracy...and while laudable efforts are being made to raise academic standards, this new and troubling deficiency is not being addressed in the standard school curriculum. As one Brooklyn teacher put it, the present emphasis in schools suggests that 'we care more about how well school children can read and write than whether they'll be alive next week.'"

> "Integrity without knowledge is weak and useless, and knowledge without integrity is dangerous and dreadful."
>
> -Samuel Johnson

Having worked in the states of Virginia and Colorado, homes to two of the worst school massacres ever to occur in this country, I can only echo the sentiments expressed by the Brooklyn teacher Goleman quotes. We do care more about test scores than whether our children and staff will be alive next week.

Money spent on school safety only increases after school tragedies but is not sustained when budgets are cut. Yet the lack of emotional intelligence is directly related to these tragedies. It does not go away. Without intervention, it continues into the next generation, and spreads just like deadly diseases without immunizations. While school shootings have taken the lives of our students and staff, poor life choices take lives in even greater numbers. Graduating students who have met all their academic requirements but are not equipped with emotional intelligence is simply unacceptable. It is time we recognize, understand, and demand change.

In honor and memory of the students that I have been privileged to work with over the years, I dedicate this book. Their names have been changed to ensure their anonymity. Each of them taught me as much as I could have ever hoped to teach them. I am better for having known them. It is with humility, gratitude, and pride I give voice to their stories.

I also dedicate this book to the following:

* My fellow colleagues whose long hours and commitment to educating our future generations are strewn with roadblocks and demands that are often unrealistic and misguided while their creativity is smothered with rigid reforms that do not make sense.

* The students who have left the halls of our schools lacking the social/

emotional skills they needed in making positive life choices....especially those whose lives were cut short because of this.

* And finally, to those who have lost their lives in our schools at the hands of other human beings who were not successfully taught to manage their emotional lives.

The Importance of Emotional Intelligence

- 7 -
My Journey

It was dark and very cold that January morning, and my nerves were a bit rattled. It would be my first day of student teaching, and I didn't want to be late. I hoped the old car I had just purchased from a shady used-car lot would start as the temperatures dipped below zero. I always hated new situations, and this one was particularly frightening as it would prove my ability to teach young children.

I had heard that Mrs. Thomas was one of the best supervising teachers a student teacher could be assigned. Yet nothing in her room was familiar to me. I really felt I would be more comfortable if the chairs were in rows and not in centers around the room. The cold and dark of the morning didn't help all my uncertainty.

I was in the final semester of my bachelor's degree at the University of Nebraska and ready to be done with college. I was not interested in the party life and was tired of having no money. I was ready to be on my own teaching. My dad had lost his job when I was a sophomore in college, and that long year of his looking for work had made me more determined to finish my degree. I managed to find a job to help with the money situation, overloaded my semesters, attended summer school each session, and now was set to complete my degree in three years instead of four.

I was a student that, by today's standards, should never have stepped foot on a four-year college campus. When I took the ACT test, I had no idea why I was up on a Saturday morning enduring it. The only thing I recall was just wanting it to be over. I am fairly certain my creative abilities came into play, and I filled in my ovals in an amazing design. I'm also fairly certain my scores were why my parents kept trying to convince me to stay at the community college in my hometown because my sister, who was four years younger, "really needed me to be close."

I scoffed at that notion and knew it was the lack of confidence in my academic ability that they were worried about. I had no idea what I wanted to do, but I had to enroll in a field of study, so I chose the teachers' college as an undecided major. I did not want to follow in the footsteps of my family, all educators, but there was some comfort in at least dipping my toe into a somewhat familiar field. I had other interests, but they were so varied that choosing the teachers' college just to get started seemed the best route. That unsure beginning quickly melted into this last semester, and now I was nearly done with my degree. I had discovered that teaching really was in my blood!

Much of my coursework seemed impractical; making game boards for students was not the real world. Just getting the students' attention and motivating them to learn was going to be the real world I would soon face. I entered my student teaching experience with very good grades in my methods courses but with complete and utter naivety about how difficult teaching was as a career.

I could not understand why students did not arrive with their Big Red notepads, large writing pencil, and box of tissues, sit down at their desk in their assigned row, and listen for the teacher's instructions. That, of course, was my experience with school. In my mind, students who didn't do this were simply "bad kids." I had no notion of why they often did not cooperate. They just needed to straighten up and behave appropriately, words that reflected my own experiences growing up.

It would be later that I would come to understand that all behavior is communication, and the bad behavior of students was a reflection of, and deeply rooted in, their tragic life stories. It was also later I realized that when I remembered the past, it was something I cherished, not repressed, as many of the children I came to know tried to do.

I remember playing Kick the Can until late in the night, swimming every summer afternoon, coming home for dinner and returning to swim until the pool closed, and then crying about how badly my eyes hurt from the hours of swimming with them open in the chlorinated pool.

"A happy childhood is one of the best gifts that parents have it in their power to bestow."

-Anonymous

I remember trips to the small town where all four of my grandparents lived. There we would beg my granddad for a ride on his horse and later chop onions, with my grandma's help, and put them in his pillowcase, knowing how much he hated onions. I remember my other grand-parent's home, my grandma's square dancing dresses, and the hamper that held the old ones she didn't wear anymore. We would dress up in them and put Herb Alpert and the Tijuana Brass on the old record player in the basement. It even had a microphone for calling a square dance that my brother often commandeered while my sister and I spun around in grand-ma's dresses on the dance floor. Imagine having grandparents with a stone fireplace and dance floor in a basement room!

I remember Easters with my cousins, and my mom wrapping my sister and my pony tails in rags so they would have long, perfect curls for church. Later in the day, we would turn the old, round, wood-en picnic table on its side and take turns getting on it trying to bal-ance and walk it around the yard. Remembering is something I am fortunate enough to do with warmth in my heart, not terror and pain. Remembering the students who have taught me so much over the years I give you........The Children Left Behind.

- 8 -
Christopher

It was below zero, but luckily my car started and I arrived at my elementary school ahead of schedule. Students started arriving, and it was clear they knew the routine of the day. They hung their coats in their designated cubbies, placed their laminated nametags in the attendance box, and then sat down at their tables. Attendance, like many of the rituals of the morning, was created by Mrs. Thomas who had spent a lifetime perfecting her teaching practices. When all the students had checked in, the tags still lying on the table were those who were absent—no need to call each student name and have them reply "here" as we had done when I went to elementary school.

There were many names to get to know and that came very quickly as different situations with the students arose. Mrs. Thomas talked to me about a few of the students with extra-special needs.

Christopher

Christopher was one of those students. He had big brown eyes, curly black hair, dimples, and a terrible temper. Christopher was mainstreamed into our regular classroom setting from the behaviorally impaired room. I was afraid of him, and he knew it, and he was only in first grade! When he was angry, he would kick over desks. Mrs. Thomas explained the many interventions Christopher had in place. He even had some mentoring outside of school by Nebraska football players and had gotten to go to the stadium on different occasions.

During my first day of student teaching, all who were new in the building that semester were meeting with the principal. He was explaining the Glasser philosophy and discipline procedures for the school and that it was expected that all those who were working with students would follow the same procedures.

It was at that moment a door flew open and out came three adults trying to remove a first grade student who was kicking and screaming "fuck you" over and over at the top of his lungs.

My heart literally raced with fear. I wanted to go back to my little neighborhood school where everyone came equipped with a Big Red writing pad and pencil, sat in rows in their desks, and played nicely together. How in the world was I to handle any of this? I was raised to behave and follow the rules. I did not understand these children robbed of their childhoods. Though I was in the last few months of my bachelor's degree, I was about to begin my real education.

Christopher taught me to understand the behaviors that drove his fury. This began with the knowledge that he had been severely beaten by his mother's boyfriend when he was four. Playing cars, building with blocks, and coloring were replaced with violence, fear, and rage. Now here he was in our classroom as long as he could handle his emotions and the other children were safe. When he became out of control, he was sent to the behaviorally impaired room with special education staff to assist him. Just keeping him calm and getting along with others seemed to be a full-time job. He was fully aware that I was afraid of his behavior and very uncertain about how to handle it.

"The secret of education lies in respecting the pupil. It is not for you to choose what he shall know, what he shall do. It is chosen and foreordained and he only holds the key to his own secret."

-Ralph Waldo Emerson

Students who were labeled "behaviorally impaired" were mainstreamed into the regular classroom as much as possible. When they became so uncontrollable they could not manage their emotions even with the support of special education staff, they would be taken to an adjoining room that contained only mats and punching bags. It was hard for me to imagine young children so full of anger they needed to be in padded rooms to release their hostilities.

When it came time for me to take over the classroom for a week, I knew I had to begin by getting a handle on Christopher because up until this point, he knew how much I relied on my supervising teacher for assistance. I asked her if she would mind letting me be completely alone with the class for the first day so I could establish my independence in the role of the classroom teacher. She kindly set up a table in the hall outside our classroom door in case her assistance was needed.

The week went by without incident, and by the end of the semester, I had developed a rapport with Christopher and no longer feared him. Christopher had developed a crush on me and was not at all happy when my Show 'n Tell came to school in the form of my fiancé! I can still see the look on his face when I broke the news of my "tell" and then introduced my fiancé, Mike, to the class; Christopher's face was less than pleased.

Shortly after Show 'n Tell time was over, the students were working in centers, and Mike had stayed to help. I will never forget walking over to the center where Christopher was by Mike's side and hearing him advise, "Wait until you see her in the morning; you will change your mind!"

Christopher further went on to ask Mike if he knew how to make a baby, and if we were going to have one, and that he could tell him how to do it if he didn't know how. Luckily for Mike, I was there to interrupt and tell young Christopher that that was not an appropriate conversation. He looked up at me sheepishly and went on to his center work.

When leaving the building that day, Christopher peeped from behind a tree as he watched us get into my car. There on the windshield he had left a note for me: "I love you, Ms. Lemons." Five years later I would see those beautiful brown eyes closed forever as he lay in a casket in the funeral home.

Christopher had taken his own life. His test scores would never matter.

The only information that I ever learned about his death was that he had gotten into an argument with his mom, and gone downstairs and hung himself with his belt. I still do not believe he truly wanted to take his life but that his anger was still unmanaged and had gotten the best of him. I have often wondered if comprehensive emotional intelligence curriculum had been a part of his education, Christopher could have thought of something different than a permanent solution to a temporary problem.

Christopher

-9-
Lindy

Lindy was Christopher's classmate. She had the adorable face of a little Sally Fields, and wore clothing that was many sizes too big and smelled of cigarette smoke. Lindy often told stories at the writing center that she never finished. A recurrent theme to these stories depicted someone entering her bedroom. Though living in a rough neighborhood, Lindy was allowed to run the streets alone from a very young age. Mrs. Thomas explained that she felt there was possible sexual abuse Lindy was attempting to convey in her stories. Social Services had been called numerous times over the years, but Lindy never could bring herself to tell about the life she was living at home. To my knowledge, nothing was done about her often wandering alone through the park across the street from her apartment even before she was school age.

The following year I was employed as a Chapter One tutor at

the school, and Lindy's second grade teacher asked me if I might be interested in mentoring Lindy since I was a part of the Big Brothers Big Sisters program at our local YMCA. She worried a great deal about Lindy's home life. I replied I would love to mentor Lindy. Soon after our conversation, Mike and I talked to her dad and asked him if we could register her for the Program and take her on some outings.

I will never forget our first trip to Lindy's apartment. She lived directly across the street from the school. I went inside to get her while Mike waited in the car. I walked into the kitchen where her dad had all the burners on the gas stove lit, I guess for heat. The walls behind the stove were soiled, probably from the stove being used in this way. As we talked for a minute, a cockroach ran between the burners and then down the side of the stove. Lindy's dad paid no attention to it.

He was an older gentleman that looked more likely to be her grandfather. Even though he was nice enough, I was very nervous and glad that he was willing to let us take Lindy out. I shuddered to think of how many more cockroaches were in the apartment, and felt sad that Lindy had to live in these conditions.

Later I would learn from a neighbor that when Lindy was three years old, she would get locked out of the apartment by her father, and the neighbor would come home to find Lindy asleep outside the apartment door. The thought of any three-year-old child in this situation still makes my heart ache. I do believe Lindy's father loved her, but his drinking problems were clearly the dominate factor in the neglect and abuse that took place in Lindy's life.

We were very broke as a newlywed couple with Mike being in dental school. We lived on my salary that was a little over seven hundred dollars a month, take-home pay, so we couldn't do things that were costly with Lindy. However, we soon realized that just taking her to a mall was an experience for her. Even though we bought very little, she loved to see all the stores and pretty things for sale.

We purchased a couple of outfits for her to wear when she was with us on weekends because her clothing was in such bad shape. I would wash what she wore to our house and send her home in clean clothes. I always felt badly that we simply didn't have the money to buy her a full wardrobe she could take home with her. Looking pretty was something she always cared about, so consequently, she loved getting cleaned up for weekend visits.

> "When you know better you do better."
>
> - Maya Angelou

We also took her on some trips to Broken Bow, Nebraska, a small town in the heart of the state where my in-laws lived. She enjoyed being a part of our extended family and getting to know them. She was inquisitive about everything because up until this time, she had lived a very sheltered life.

My father-in-law, Jack, owned and managed a small meat packing plant. I will never forget on one trip, Lindy wanted to see a cow slaughtered. Mike and I talked with her about whether or not she really would want to see such a thing and tried to be certain she wouldn't be traumatized by the experience. She urged us to let her see what happened behind the scenes and so, against our better judgment, we went to see the beginning stages of meat processing! I am not sure what Lindy recalls of this event, but I clearly remember the dead cow hanging from its hooves and a quick slit that was made all the way down its middle section with various liquids and organs spilling out. I have to say, I'm surprised I still eat meat!

I felt very queasy about this time, but not Lindy; she thought it was all very cool. We did not stay long after that feeling she had seen enough, but she would have happily stayed for all of it.

Lindy also really wanted to see the cadaver lab where some of Mike's dental classes were held. We tried again to be sure she was ready for this, but clearly this young mind wanted to know all about the cadavers and what Mike had been learning in school.

Off we went to the smelly lab and again, I was the queasy one with Lindy eagerly absorbing it all. Only a small portion of the body was uncovered by a sheet, so we could just see part of the arm. Lindy exclaimed, "It looks like chicken meat!"

I had to agree with her. Again, I am surprised I still eat meat! She was definitely a sponge when it came to learning all she could about the world.

The first thing she always did after arriving at our house was freshen up. I remember one Friday evening the following year while on a weekend visit to our house, Lindy seemed nervous and hurriedly got ready to go out to eat. She had plugged her curling iron in, and I was trying to help her curl her hair. I ran my hands through her bangs, and she jumped as I hit a small, bruised bump on her head. I asked her what had happened, and she said she had bumped her head on the wall of her apartment earlier that day. I didn't press her about it because she seemed on edge. She calmed down once we were out for pizza later that evening. I was concerned about the origin of her bump.

Later that year while on a visit, Lindy was upset because Social Services had, once again, come to school to talk to her. She told me she had asked them what would happen to her if they took her away from her dad. She said they told her she would be placed in a foster home. She said she didn't want to go to a foster home.

It was late that evening as I told her the unknown is always scary, but it was important to tell Social Services if her safety was at risk. I assured her that we would support her. It took great courage and many tears for Lindy to admit that her dad had abused her. Three hours later, we stopped talking and tried to get some sleep.

First thing in the morning, I called the police and was told to bring her to the station. We were there all morning as she attempted to tell the police what she had told me the night before. The officer made a call to Social Services and informed them that Mike and I agreed to keep Lindy until other arrangements could be made. In the end, Lindy lived with us for about three months as a temporary foster child.

After leaving the police station that Saturday, we went home to get a few things in place for Lindy. Mike searched the basement of our home where we had some items in a small storage room.

We had unexpectedly purchased the home where we were renting the main level apartment. While I was working at a clothing retail store, my manager, who owned the house, informed us they wanted to sell it and wondered if we might be interested. With Mike in dental school, we never dreamed of owning a home, but we were able to get special first-time home-owner financing and put very little down to buy it. So we became property owners, apartment managers, and now foster parents, just as un-expectantly.

Mike emerged from the basement with a small, old, living room table and antique mirror that needed resilvering for Lindy's bedroom. He hung the mirror and put the table below it. I took Lindy to the store and we got a few things like hand lotion for her. The lotion sticks in my mind because her hands were always dry and rough when she had visited us.

She was thrilled with her "new" room. I was reminded how much I had taken for granted in my life, like a bottle of hand lotion. Lindy set her brush, comb, and lotion on the old table neatly. She repeatedly admired herself in the mirror and rearranged the items on the table.

It was spring, and I was teaching in a town about forty minutes away. When I was offered the contract to teach first grade, I was also asked what I wanted to coach. I didn't coach, but it was clear that I would if I wanted to teach! I told them girls' junior high track would probably be the best fit since I had at least run some track when I had been in school.

Now we had an instant family, and I was leaving the house before seven in the morning and getting home around seven at night and knew of no babysitters to help us out. Luckily, one of my co-workers, Jenny, mentioned the situation to her mom. It also happened that Jenny's dad was the minister of the church we attended, and so her mom quickly went into action getting help from congregation members. We had an entire wardrobe at our house for Lindy within a couple of days.

Additionally, Jenny's mom volunteered to pick up Lindy early in the morning before Mike left for dental school. She fed Lindy breakfast and took her to school. Later in the day, she picked her up from school and took her to their home until Mike returned home. Lindy bonded quickly to Jenny's mom and was grateful for the stability she added to her life. We too, were so thankful to have such a loving person help us with Lindy.

While living with us, there were two things Lindy did repeatedly. One was to put on the cassette tape made of our wedding and listen to it as she slowly turned the pages of our wedding album, and the second was to watch the movie *Dirty Dancing*. She loved both of these rituals she had created for herself during this unsure time in her life.

There were some disturbing times in those months. Lindy's mom was still alive and living in a halfway house. Lindy was placed with her father after her mom had chased Lindy and her father around the house with a knife. Her mom suffered from schizophrenia. When she randomly called our home, it was frightening since we didn't know anything about her situation or stability. There were many sleepless nights as we got closer to Lindy's trial date.

Before the trial, Lindy's guardian ad litem and another Social Service worker met with us and showed Lindy the court room. They explained where she would sit when on the stand and where her dad would be during the trial. Lindy was very nervous and said she didn't want to see her dad. The workers explained she could just look straight ahead and did not need to look over at the table where he would be seated. It was sad to watch her endure another round of questioning and difficult to understand why a tape of her testimony could not be taken to court instead. I was so out of my comfort zone, and again realized how sheltered from the real world I had always been.

On trial day, our minister and his wife accompanied us for support.

Lindy was put on the witness stand, and I will always have etched in my memory her attempts to avoid looking at her dad. She again told her painful story. This was difficult and confusing because she still loved her dad.

She was about halfway into her testimony when, out of the blue, her dad slammed his hand down onto the table, looked over at us, and yelled, "They told her to say that!"

Everyone in the courtroom jumped from this frightening outburst. My heart was racing as I rushed with others to the witness stand where Lindy had dissolved into tears.

There was a door just off of the witness stand where we quickly whisked Lindy. Whoever it was sitting at a desk quickly left so we could try to calm Lindy. She sobbed as she kept saying, "You said he wasn't supposed to say anything."

The court officials tried to explain that he wasn't supposed to say anything, and tried, again, to convince her he would have to be quiet, or the judge would deal with him. It took some time to get Lindy emotionally prepared to go back to the witness stand and attempt to finish her testimony.

At that point, I was so frustrated by a system that allowed the re-victimization of a young child. I was also scared out of my mind and trying not to let Lindy see my fear. The defense attorney was worse than any fictional court drama lawyer I had ever seen on television. When he had the chance to cross examine poor Lindy, he requested, in a harsh, short manner, that she tell a lie. She didn't understand, so he kept repeating the demand.

Finally, Lindy complied, and told a lie by saying, "Jill Doty is not my Y Pal." Lindy and I were "Y Pals" with the local YMCA Big Brother/ Big Sister Program. Of course he couldn't wait to use that in his closing arguments when he declared, "She is a proven liar, as we saw today."

We all gasped at this ridiculous argument. Of all the stressful, fearful experiences in my life, being on the witness stand ranks at the top of the list. The defense attorney was going to try to discredit me since I was considered the only real witness to the crime. It turned out the weekend I discovered the bump on her head was one piece of corroboration they could use in the case. Knowing my testimony could have a dramatic effect on the life a child was extremely stressful.

My cross examination took over an hour and a half. The defense attorney tried to get me to admit to "cueing" Lindy as to what to say on the stand. And again, he couldn't wait to mention in his closing arguments that even monkeys can be taught do things on cue.

While I understand everyone deserves a defense, this man went far beyond providing that service. There was no other way to describe him than as a cruel, unsympathetic, human being. In the hallways on break, he sauntered up to us and said, "I can't believe you people are putting this child through this. You are never going to win."

Luckily, Lindy was with a court worker and didn't hear his totally unnecessary comment. There was no jury for this trial, and we felt great distress that we only had a timid law student with his supervisor to represent Lindy. In the end, the judge believed Lindy. We sighed in relief when he read his verdict. Lindy's father was ordered into counseling. Lindy was to continue in counseling and foster care until the time her father completed his mandated counseling.

He never completed this, so Lindy would never live with him again. Lindy's half- sister had contacted us immediately after she found out what had happened and wanted Lindy to come live with her family.

The courts had found records indicating that when Lindy's adult sister was younger, there were also allegations of abuse by their shared father. However, charges were never filed, so the case wasn't prosecuted. Social Services asked that her sister complete some counseling before Lindy could live with her. So, we spent about three months as foster parents, and I concluded a very busy and unexpected school year....coaching track and all! I should give credit to my sister for stepping in as a substitute coach the day we were in court with Lindy. It was the only track meet our girls won that season!

Lindy went to live with her sister later that spring and stayed there until she reached junior high. We had our first child, Katie, a few years later. I remember thinking how protective I felt of Katie and would think of little Lindy at a very young age running the park alone in her previous neighborhood. When Katie was three, I remembered Lindy's neighbor telling me of finding Lindy asleep outside her apartment door, locked out. Having my own child deepened my feelings of sadness at this neglect.

We moved to Southwest Nebraska when Mike finished dental school. Lindy stayed in touch through letters and every once in awhile, phone calls. Her teen years were difficult, and when things weren't going so well with her sister, she moved out to stay with a friend from elementary school.

Later, while she was in high school, I got letters from Lindy telling me how her friend had gotten into drugs. She wanted to know if I thought she should tell someone. I was always amazed how Lindy kept herself out of trouble and wanted to do the right thing.

Then in her senior year of high school, her dad became ill with cancer. Lindy had a strong faith in God and a very forgiving spirit. She had forgiven her father for his abuse and took him into the home of her friend, where she was living, to care for him in his last days. He died with Lindy at his side. I will never forget her letter outlining how she had taken care of him until the end. She had yet to graduate from high school.

Learning a set of facts to pass a test is not a priority for a child searching for a safe place to call home.

While Lindy was a good student, her test scores would never measure her strength, resiliency, and all she had overcome while attempting to make sense of the abuse she had endured. Today, Lindy is a grown woman with a husband and two children.

On a visit to Colorado a few summers ago, Lindy's two children were having fun playing in my basement creating planes and other things with the Lego set. Their dad was with them building things and having a good time. I had put together some goody bags for them and my nephew who had come over to meet them. The adults were all out on the deck when I gave the three kids their goody bags. Lindy's oldest son looked up while they were in the midst of digging through their bags to see all they contained and said, "Thank you, Jill."

His sister and my nephew also thanked me. It is a point worth telling because over the years, the most important attribute I've found in those who overcome life's obstacles is a **grateful heart**.

I teach a lesson on "Attitude" to my high school freshmen each year. We start by talking about when life isn't fair and how we all encounter such circumstances. During these times, we become "walking wounded" because we are hurt and searching for meaning. We discuss those who never leave this stage but always remain a **victim** to life's circumstances and then contrast it with those, who through their resiliency, move on to become "wounded healers."

We are all "walking wounded" when bad things happen and life isn't fair, yet we have the individual choice about how we let it affect us. Gratitude and grace define the "wounded healers" I have had the privilege of knowing. There are many examples of people who not only move through difficulty, but use it for good.

I will never forget my first meeting with Dave Pelzer who wrote his first book, *A Child Called It*, which detailed his abuse at the hands of his mother, when he was a child in the seventies. His case would later be called one of the worst child abuse cases in the state of California.

We had just moved to Virginia after I completed my master's degree in counseling at the University of Nebraska in Kearney. I found out Dave was going to speak back in Nebraska at the State Counselors Convention in the fall. I really wanted to hear what he had to say, so we flew back to attend a football game and the convention in Lincoln. My father was in his final year before retiring as a school counselor, and also attended the convention.

My prediction was that Dave would highlight the need for society to improve social services for children based on his own experiences of being left in an abusive home for many years before he was "rescued," as he termed it in his book. However, that was not the point of his keynote address.

There sat hundreds of counselors around tables in a ballroom at the Cornhusker Hotel mesmerized as Dave recounted his terrible abuse. He often slipped into other personas by imitating famous people such as Arnold Schwarzenegger. It seemed to be the only way he was able to tell us about his painful memories. While reading his book, I had to put it down and release audible sighs just to get through it. I could not fathom the challenge of standing in front of this large audience and trying to convey his own painful stories. It is unthinkable that a mother could stab her own child and then not get any medical treatment for him. Just as sickening is a father who knows his child has been stabbed and is oozing with infection, and yet does nothing to help him.

Dave related his horrific memories and then described his "rescue." When Dave reached the main point of his keynote address, you could have heard a pin drop in that ballroom of counselors. He simply said, "Thank you; thank you for all you do to rescue children."

I doubt many were without lumps in their throats and tears in their eyes. His message was to thank us, with no hint of wanting sympathy for his terrible life. He used his life story as an inspiration to others, and exemplified "the indomitable human spirit!" From that point, I paid attention to gratitude as a trait in survivors of life's unfair circumstances.

A few years later, I got to hear Dave again at the American School Counselor Convention in Miami. I had begun using his book when doing elementary guidance lessons, only telling what I thought young children were old enough to process, but making sure that I pointed out his message of survival. My fourth and fifth grade students each made a page in a book I presented to him, explaining what his story had meant to each of them.

Now in my home all these years later, noting how Lindy's grateful heart had been passed down to her children, I was so pleased. She had made a choice to break the chain of abuse in her family and instead, she passed down something good.

To this day, Lindy thanks me for being her "guardian angel." She has never stopped thanking me for taking her in when she needed help. What she doesn't realize is that I am a better person because of Lindy. She taught me to be thankful for the life I have lived.

– 10 –

Anna

After student teaching, I taught in the same school for a year and then moved on for a year to the consolidated rural school where I coached track. I then went back to teach in Lincoln, Nebraska.

I was busy preparing for another day of school when Jane, a fellow teacher, appeared at my classroom door clearly upset. "Anna's been hurt. She's in the cafeteria having her breakfast. It looks like she has been beaten. Her nose looks broken."

Again, I was reminded of the wonderful gift my parents had given me – a "childhood." Until I started teaching, I didn't realize how precious it was. I was allowed to be the child rather than the parent. I was sheltered from the world's tragedies which was easier back then with the absence of cyberspace, text messaging, facebook, emails, and instant messaging.

Being so sheltered made this moment extra difficult; one of my second grade students was in the cafeteria, and it appeared she had been beaten. My university text books and professors did not come close to preparing me for this day. I tried to calm Jane by telling her the best thing for Anna would be for us to stay composed. If she had been beaten, she didn't need us to make a scene. I asked Jane to let her come to class as it was time for the bell, anyway, and I would get her to the nurse.

"As a child I believed with all of my heart that if I could survive my ordeal, then not only could I accomplish what I set my mind to but anything else I would encounter had to be easier. This is why my story is not about my being a victim of child abuse, but of the indomitable human spirit within us all."

-Dave Pelzer, A Man Named Dave

It was library day, so the students put their attendance tags in the basket, got their library books, and sat in the circle on the rug while I recorded the attendance and lunch count. Anna came in quietly with her head down, checked in, and sat on the rug with her book. She had pretty brown eyes, but we rarely saw them. Her wild, untamed hair, which always had dead remnants of lice eggs, was routinely checked by the nurse, and concealed a great deal of her face. I saw the redness, swelling, and small cut across the bridge of her nose.

I finished the attendance and sent it off with the office helper and glanced back down at Anna. Her small body, crouched Indian style, shook as she clutched her library book. I reminded myself to breathe deeply, blink away any sign of tears, and then got Tom, the teacher from next door, to step in for a moment. I wanted someone other than just Jane and I to witness Anna's state.

68

Tom glanced into the room and immediately stepped back into the hallway. "You've got to get her to the nurse," he said. Tears filled his eyes.

I explained I was going to walk the class to the library and then quietly take her to the nurse. So far, the other students hadn't noticed Anna's face. I took her hand in line as we went to the library, and it seemed she was reassured that I knew she needed help. When we arrived at the nurse's office, I kept hold of her hand and bent down telling her I thought that maybe the nurse needed to look at her nose. She nervously told me it was okay, but ultimately agreed to come with me.

Though this happened over twenty-five years ago, those next few hours are still etched deeply into my memory as are all emotionally charged events. Jane had forewarned the nurse about the situation. The nurse carefully looked at Anna's nose and asked her how she hurt it and if she was hurt anywhere else. Anna's body and voice both shook as she replied that she didn't know. The nurse lifted her hair and behind each ear we saw more wounds—red, cut-like marks that followed the curves of the backs of her ears.

Again, the nurse asked what happened, and this time Anna said the mosquitoes must have gotten her. Her demeanor and illogical reasons for the wounds were further evidence someone had done this to her.

My few years of experience had already taught me we were sunk if she wouldn't tell us if the wounds were caused by abuse. She would have to go back to a home that clearly was not safe. Even if she did tell us she had gotten the wounds from someone in her home, she could still be forced to return.

It is a noble thing to want to preserve the family; it often just isn't the right thing. If the family members were all sick with a serious, contagious disease, we wouldn't try to keep everyone together. We would separate them and try to heal each individual so they wouldn't continue to re-infect each other. But many don't comprehend how contagious abuse is, and that the cure takes far more time, motivation by family members, and effort than our social systems can begin to absorb. Thus, the cycle often continues, and the next generation bears the scars as the illness is passed on.

I went to our Lost and Found box and retrieved a sweater for Anna. Hopefully, the added warmth would calm her a bit. I'm not sure who called the police, but they soon appeared. We did not have school counselors in the early eighties and sadly, in today's world the elementary counselor is considered the most expendable employee. No one thinks of the young children like Anna who come to school day after day needing additional support.

These memories are why I write.

These moments from my past still haunt me every time I hear of budget cuts and realize how little we do to serve the emotional needs of our students. These moments make me want to cry out to our lawmakers about the costs of ignoring emotional intelligence. It should be the number one priority of education, for as I learned as a young teacher, the rest will come if we begin with the affective domain.

There is a reason our prisons are overcrowded; we simply do not comprehend things that do not fit into spreadsheets and pie charts. In a class I teach, I challenge students to find news stories that reflect emotional intelligence. From the greedy CEOs and Madoffs of the world, to the heroes that endlessly work helping others, it has nothing to do with how individuals scored on standardized tests or their grade point averages from high school. Rather, it has everything to do with their level of emotional intelligence.

The nurse, principal, Anna, police officer, and I sat around a table. The officer calmly put his hand on Anna's little hand as he said, "Anna, I need to know what happened to you, Honey, and I need you to tell me the truth."

I thought, *Here we go; she is going to tell him the mosquitoes got her.* There was a brief moment of silence and then she replied, "My daddy did it."

"Children are our most valuable natural resource."

-Anonymous

Breathe, keep breathing, blink, just blink, swallow, swallow hard—the lump wouldn't go away, and I uttered a silent prayer of thanks to God; she was going to tell the truth. We might be able to save her from the hell she called home.

Very little more was asked at that point. The officer explained that we needed to take her to the hospital to ensure she was okay. She started to cry and said she didn't want to go without me. I asked the principal to get Jane to cover my class so I could go with Anna. She rode with the officer, and I followed in my car.

At the hospital, Anna's face and ear wounds were examined and cleaned. She was asked to undress and put on a gown so the doctor could check the rest of her body. Her bottom showed further bruising. I felt my efforts at trying to keep my emotions in check starting to wane. I could not imagine the cruelty Anna had endured. When the x-rays began, I explained to Anna that since I couldn't be in the room, I was going to use the restroom and get a drink of water, and I'd be back in just a few minutes.

I quickly looked for a pay phone. I just needed someone to reassure me for a moment. I called Mike at dental school. He asked why I was calling in the middle of the day. I explained I just needed to hear his voice and told him I was at the hospital with a student who had come to school severely abused. We talked briefly but enough for me to garner the strength needed for what lay ahead.

When I returned to Anna, we were left in a room for what seemed like hours. I'm sure that Social Services had already been notified by the school nurse, and now they were consulting with doctors, etc. to figure out what to do next. I told Anna I thought she would probably go to a foster home that evening.

She, as are all children, was afraid of the unknown. This is why so many choose to remain silent; the unknown seems even more frightening. I told her that I thought they were trying to find her the best foster mom ever, and that she would probably cook her a hot, delicious dinner that night, and she would be safe. Silently I prayed, *Please, please let the system work for her, and let my words become reality for Anna.*

Finally, a social worker arrived and explained to Anna she was going to a foster home. Anna's eyes reflected the fear she felt. I explained to the social worker that I had told Anna I felt certain she was going to a wonderful foster mom. The social worker smiled and said, "I do have a wonderful mom for you."

After many long hours, I left the hospital. Anna had gone to her foster home for the evening. I have no memory of the rest of that day. I'm sure I went home and collapsed from the emotional exhaustion. Anna did not return to school for a few days as she needed both emotional and physical recovery time.

At some point I learned that when the police arrived to arrest her father, he confessed to everything. Thankfully, there was some hope that Anna would not be returned home. Anna's dad and step-mom both took part in Anna's abuse. Anna was not allowed to use the restroom, and when she subsequently lost control of her bladder on the floor, she was picked up by her ears and her nose was rubbed into the carpet where she had urinated. I couldn't begin to imagine the horrific emotional pain that must have accompanied her physical injuries.

Learning a set of facts for a test was the least of Anna's worries that day.

All the piles of curriculum packed with learning objectives do not matter when the ones you depend on for love and support have broken your mind, body, and spirit.

Despite my youth and inexperience, I knew enough to set the curriculum aside for awhile and focus on lessons that were not in the books. We held a class meeting the next day so I could explain to the others that Anna needed me the day before which was why I did not return to get them from the library. They wanted all the details. I told them that what they needed to know was that Anna was living in a very nice foster home and would need lots of warm fuzzies, no cold prickles, from each of them when she returned. I carefully explained that they were not to ask her questions, but if she talked about what happened with them, they simply needed to listen and tell her they were sorry.

We were a team and had spent a great deal of time learning about relationships: how to be a friend, resolve conflicts, talk things out, listen, and most of all, how to care about each other. My students knew my absolute rule that no one made fun of anyone else. It was a line not to be crossed, and we had spent much time learning why.

When Anna returned to school, we saw her face fully for the first time all year. Her wonderful, loving foster mom had worked on her hair for over three hours, carefully pulling out every louse egg from each hair shaft. She then pulled her hair into two pony tails high on her head using hair bands embellished with bright, red, marble-like balls. Anna wore a never-seen-before smile as she excitedly said, "You were right, Mrs. Doty. My foster mom is a really good cook, and she makes me the best food."

Again, I silently prayed another prayer of thanksgiving! I was so grateful that Anna had been placed in a loving foster home because not all of them are better places for children.

The benefits of our class meeting were seen that first day when Anna returned to school. Her classmates went on about their work without making her feel the center of unwanted attention. At the appropriate times, I would see a student go out of their way to help her with a task and offer their friendship. In a few weeks, I had some students come to me to quietly complain they had seen Anna being mean to our class hamster. This was, of course, further indication of her brutal life. It became an important life lesson for her classmates. All behavior is communication.

Anna's trial day came, and for the second time in my short career, the need for me to testify. With her father having confessed, it is difficult for me to remember why we had to go to trial. I recalled the vivid memories of sitting on a witness stand, being cross-examined, and the severe anxiety.

My experience with the defense attorney from Lindy's trial made me all the more nervous. It is extremely difficult to keep calm enough to notice when the lawyer is manipulating the facts. Ultimately, you never want to feel that something you said may be mischaracterized, resulting in a child being sent back home and subjected to further abuse. "Pressure" understates my emotions that day. Once again, I felt that my testimony was going to be significant because no one else from the school was called. The only other witness was the police officer.

Pictures of the backs of Anna's ears had been taken while we were still at school that day in the nurse's office. While on the witness stand, I was asked to state if I recognized them. I indicated that I did and that I had been present when they were taken. Later during cross-examination, though the defense attorney was kinder than the one at Lindy's trial, he still worked to discredit my testimony. It was nothing short of the grace of God that kept me level-headed as the attorney went from picture to picture showing the cuts and bruises on Anna's body while he asked if they could have been similar ones on another child. These pictures only showed close-up images of her injuries. I sat for what seemed eternity thinking how to answer this.

It is difficult to describe the fury one feels when witnessing injuries caused to an innocent child. I did not want to be forced to agree that this could have been another child. NO, NO, NO, kept running through my head as I sat contemplating the question.

I had been there through every painful moment, fighting the tears, trying to be calm for Anna as each injury was revealed. These were her injuries, and I did not want to be manipulated into saying these injuries could have been on another child!

Then I noticed something familiar in a picture, and felt a surge of triumph in my heart as I told them, "No, this could not be another child with similar injuries because these pictures showed the sweater we had taken out of the Lost and Found to keep her warm that morning!"

As I said the words, I thought, *Thank you God; Thank you God for helping me to notice the sweater!*

I feel like I'm writing a screen play, but it is not. Each moment was real and still makes me cry all these years later. Anna's case was won, and she would never be returned to her abusive home. Some years later I heard that a couple, both teachers with Lincoln Public Schools, had filed for her adoption.

– 11 –
Stressful Times

The year teaching Anna's class was one of the most challenging years of my life. I recorded many of the events in a journal I kept for my daughter, Katie. The journal had been a gift from Mrs. Thomas, my student teaching supervisor. Her deep beliefs in teaching students to write were instilled in me during that semester we worked together. She told me I wouldn't remember it all if I didn't journal, and she was right. The baby books I kept don't come close to capturing life so long ago.

I still become emotional when I read segments of the journal from that challenging time. In October that year, my in-laws had come for a visit. While staying with us, they went to the dental school to have Mike clean and examine their teeth. This would be the last time we saw my father-in-law as he passed away a few weeks later of a sudden heart attack.

Mike was one month away from his National Board exams. No matter your age, test objectives and materials mean little when you've just lost your father. To this day, I am amazed that he was able to pass his comprehensive exams, but attribute it to his strong desire to fulfill his father's dream that his son become a dentist.

The Sunday evening we received the news of my father-in-law's death, I went to school to prepare a week of lesson plans. Letting myself in through a dark, back doorway to my school, I wondered how to help the substitute understand the many unique situations in my very diverse class of well over twenty students.

Unfortunately, these students had already had experience with a substitute when, in the middle of September, I had gotten the stomach flu that kept me from school for four days. I rarely missed work, so this was highly unusual. Now I needed to miss an entire week to cope with my father-in-law's death.

Little did I know that Anna's tragedy was still to unfold along with another trial in which to testify. On top of all this, Katie would end up hospitalized in an oxygen tent suffering from an upper respiratory infection. I had missed so many days of school that year that by spring semester, it was easier for Mike to stay home with Katie when she became ill than for me to miss more work.

I came home one day to find the house empty. I knew Mike was going to take Katie to the doctor, a decision he had made because she was getting sicker by the hour. I called the doctor's office, and they informed me that they sent Katie to the hospital.

I was horrified. I rushed to the hospital, and when I finally found her room, I was in tears. Walking through the door didn't help. There was my sweet little girl lying in an oxygen tent, her eyes red and puffy from all the crying—or later, as her dad would tell me—screaming she had done that afternoon.

Mike looked equally exhausted and upset. He explained that they wanted to x-ray Katie's chest, and that it required her to stand in a position with her arms straight above her head for a long time. She screamed the entire time. When they were sent to the hospital, the x-rays were repeated and she had to endure it all again. Looking back, I truly wonder how we survived so many cumulative stresses in such a short time.

When real life is occurring in such stressful situations, taking standardized tests over memorized materials is difficult. Then, when the scores are used to make assumptions about how effective a teacher is and how well a student is learning without any further information, it is inaccurate and unfair.

The score is like a small piece of a jigsaw puzzle from the very corner edge. There are so many more pieces, and it is the important pieces in the middle that reveal the true picture. Those middle pieces represent real-life learning that is occurring and certainly put the small corner test score piece into perspective. As I previously stated, even a good test score tells us very little that predicts a student's success in life.

In his book *Standardized Minds*, Peter Sacks outlines the research on standardized testing. He states, "When researchers have asked the even more basic question of how well standardized test scores predict one's eventual success in the workplace, correlations all but disappear. At best, high test scores are pretty good indicators of participation in professions such as law, medicine, or university teaching, for which one must make certain standardized test cutoff to enter a required academic program. But test scores tell us little about someone's real-world capabilities in medi-cine, law, or teaching. In short, scoring high on standardized tests is a good predictor of one's ability to score high on standardized tests. Evidence strong-ly suggests that standardized testing flies in the face of recent advances in our understanding of how people learn to think and reason. Repeatedly in the research over the past few years, especially in the grade school arena (K-12), one finds evidence that traditional tests reinforce passive, rote learn-ing of facts and formulas, quite contrary to the active, critical thinking skills many educators now believe schools should be encouraging. Many suspect that the speeded, multiple-choice tests are themselves powerful in-centives for compartmentalized and superficial learning."

> *"Bodily exercise, when compulsory, does no harm to the body; but knowledge which is acquired under compulsion obtains no hold on the mind."*
>
> -Plato

So why do we spend so much time and money on these tests?

There are no footnotes to explain all the things (pieces of the puzzle) that may affect a score. If there were, we would often reframe our percep-tion of the scores. When you understand the lives of many children, it is sometimes hard to believe they score as well as they do. Conversely, you sometimes wonder how other students, who score so high, flounder in coping with the real world.

- 12 -
Gabe and Bobby

Gabe and Bobby were two students that required great amounts of time and attention that same fateful year. Gabe lived with his grandmother, and there was no one in his life to give him attention and care. I do not recall where his parents were, nor do I remember why he was living with his grandmother. What I do remember is how much he needed attention. There were so many days I felt there was simply not enough of me to go around.

One day as we were lining up to go home, Gabe misbehaved in line. I very rarely kept students after school, but I told him to sit down and wait for me to walk the other students out, and then we would discuss his behavior. In my mind, I can still see his face when I walked back into the room. His grin spread from ear-to-ear. I couldn't help but smile back at him as I commented, "Gabe, it looks to me like staying after school is something you are enjoying!"

He kept grinning and shook his head, yes. He had no one waiting for him at home. He, like Lindy, often ran the neighborhood alone for hours. Most of the time when his behavior landed him in the time out chair, he would wail, "I wish I were dead."

After seeing his smiling face that day after school, I proposed the idea that we make a special coupon to put in our coupon basket. I randomly called out students for good behavior, and told them to mark a point on our classroom chart. After five points, they got to pick a coupon. Their favorite one was for "twenty minutes of free choice time" and could be redeemed whenever they wanted.

This single management technique got more students on task and working than any other I tried while teaching. I loved watching their little faces when students would bring me their coupon and say they wanted their twenty minutes of free time. Then they would proceed to get out the Play-doh, or perhaps paints, or play a game from the shelf while the rest of the class was working.

On this particular day, Gabe and I went to the coupon basket, took a few blank coupons, and filled them in with "twenty minutes after school with Mrs. Doty." We changed staying after school from a negative situa-

"Boys learn to wear the mask so skillfully—in fact, they don't even know they are doing it— that it can be difficult to detect what is really going on when they are suffering at school, when their friendships are not working out, when they are being bullied, becoming depressed, even dangerously so, to the point of feeling suicidal."

-William Pollack, Ph.D.,

Real Boys

tion and replaced it with something Gabe greatly wanted and needed-undivided attention. Now he worked for what he needed instead of getting attention any way possible. Since pointing out good behavior was random to prevent students always expecting rewards for doing what was right, I had to purposely watch Gabe to catch him a bit more that first week so he earned enough points to get his prized coupon.

He was so excited to stay after school. He helped me take down a bulletin board, carefully removing the tape from the items so they could be returned. Gabe happily put students' work into their cubbies. Then Mike showed up to say "hi" on his way to the corner car wash. He asked Gabe if he would like to come with him.

Though I would be apprehensive in today's world for legal reasons, I agreed to let him go because Gabe was so eager. When they returned, Gabe was beside himself from all the attention in one afternoon. Mike later told me that Gabe examined the buttons on the car and kept repeating, "Yeah man, this is bad; this is a bad car!"

Of course, it meant that our little, used hatchback Honda impressed him!

Then there was Bobby. ADHD was not a term you heard much back then, but if there ever was a child who suffered from Attention Deficit Hyperactive Disorder, it was Bobby. He never seemed to stop moving; I often wondered if he slept at night. In addition, he had anger issues that flared up when he didn't get his way. One day while arguing with a classmate, he stood up and kicked over a desk. As a young teacher, this room full of needy children frequently overwhelmed me during those moments.

Luckily, I worked with a phenomenal staff and asked for help from our multidisciplinary team regarding Bobby. The team was composed of both special education and regular education teachers, many who had years of experience with different interventions. This was the mid-eighties. Today RtI—Response to Intervention—is the newest pendulum swing in education. Call it something new and it appears we are doing something innovative. I love fresh ideas, but sometimes best practices haven't changed. We sometimes discount our experienced teachers who have weathered the storms in education!

Our team produced ideas for me to try with Bobby. Since he was untrained in sitting still for any length of time, we decided to start in small increments. I taped a square around his desk which allowed several feet in all directions for him to move about when he needed to. He had to stay within the designated square, preventing him from traveling around the room and disrupting others.

While I held reading groups, I also had to time him. Each time he stayed in his seat for ten minutes, he got a few M&M's. It amazed me that the others didn't complain about not getting M&M's, but we had discussed Bobby's plan in a class meeting so they were aware he would be receiving treats. Timing him every ten minutes while I also held reading groups was incredibly difficult. However, the team had advised that it would get better as the time increments increased.

It was amazing how well this behavior management worked. Very quickly Bobby was completely weaned from the M&M's, and eventually, he was able to stay seated for longer periods of time. We were even able to remove the tape from the floor.

This was just one student. The amount of time needed to meet, discuss, create, and implement a plan was immense. Those who do not work in education can't imagine how much is expected on any given day in our schools. I believe there must be a special place in heaven for elementary teachers with unending preps and student needs.

On more than a few occasions, I have heard people say teaching is an easy profession and further comment on the long summer breaks. Many do not realize that teachers are not paid for those breaks. Rather, their salaries are amortized over the summer. Quite honestly, I am not certain I could stay in education without the summer breaks. Only those who are in education can truly understand the intensity and stress of working in public education.

Of course, some teachers are not as affected by stress. They are the masters of the worksheet. Education reforms do not bother these individuals. Affected are our finest who take their responsibilities to heart. They are the ones who go the extra mile and give up their lunches and after school time to tutor students. They are also the ones who care enough to listen to students.

They know and understand what many students bring to school from their home lives. They understand the value of the "relationship" and the need for genuine concern and compassion. They also know success isn't about giving students a "free" ride; rather, they hold them accountable for their actions. They understand that

> "True teachers are those who use themselves as bridges over which they invite their students to cross; then, having facilitated their crossing, joyfully collapse, encouraging them to create their own."
>
> -Nikos Kazantzakis

"rescuing" and "enabling" do not empower students to deal with the challenges in life. They are heroes and role models for students who need a place where they are cared about, made to feel significant, and find belonging.

- 13 -
Real Life Lessons

Somehow I made it through those first rocky years of teaching, and Mike managed to pass his dental boards despite the gripping grief from his father's sudden death. We moved across the state to start a dental practice after his graduation. We were now faced with all the lessons that weren't taught in the schools we had attended: how to keep a marriage together in the midst of so many stresses; how to run a business; and how to grieve well. Despite my graduating in three years instead of four, and his graduating from professional school in the midst of tragedy, we still had no idea what to do. We now had to rely on our common sense and emotional intelligence to see us through.

In some ways we did very well, and in others, we did not. I did not teach during this time but instead helped Mike establish his business. Now we were suddenly employers. We discovered that employees could be very skilled but squander it because of their inability to "play nice in the sandbox!"

We paid well over ten thousand dollars to a consultant to teach us how to create a successful business. A small segment of this training focused on important financial statistics to monitor the health of the practice, and the rest of training centered on emotional intelligence skills. Communication skills were the main focal point of the training. It was excellent consulting, but it amazed me that what seemed as basic as learning the ABC's had never been taught to either of us in all our years of education. Now we were paying a premium price for it!

These years provided me with further evidence of what happens when we do not allow children to simply "play" with each other; we harm their emotional development. We put children into organized sports well before they are developmentally ready with the adults in charge. We cut out recess in elementary schools to allow more time learning classroom objectives that are supposedly the ultimate indicators of success. And we reduce availability of electives such as physical education and industrial and fine arts, qualifying them as low-priority standards. Hence, we eliminate the "play" that provides rehearsal for developing relationship skills.

When I was not immersed in teaching, I saw clearly the need for educational reforms because now I had a different perspective. I understood why employers beg schools to teach students "how to get along with each other."

Our second child, Drew was born during this time. I was very grateful that I was not teaching with the enormous demands and stresses that I had when Katie was a baby. I kept my teaching certificate current by taking the necessary continuing education between renewal periods.

At the urging of my parents, I took a class that they had taken and highly recommended called "Developing Capable People" based on Stephen Glenn's book *Raising Self Reliant Children in a Self-Indulgent World*. It was not the habit of my parents to take classes, but they had heard this one was exceptional.

Since it was in my field and would help me renew my teaching license, I signed up to take the class. Afterwards, I echoed what my parents and others were saying: Why didn't we learn this stuff in college? *Why doesn't everyone have to take a course like this one?*

In his book, Glenn discusses how education changed when the baby boomers hit school. Suddenly, we needed to educate the masses, and to do this, everything became "standardized." "Standardized" is a mold into which everyone must fit and, as a friend of mine from Tennessee once said, no child left behind, and no child gets ahead. With the shift from the little one house schoolroom to standardized education the sad consequences in education began.

Glenn outlined these changes stating, "Overnight educators threw together what was later described as 'a maladaptive response to a crisis situation,' and called it public education. In the subsequent thirty years, data suggests that makeshift solutions worked for very few students and actually proved deleterious for most. They were bad also for teachers. On the students' side, there was a marked increase in the drop-out rate and other forms of resistance to education. Despite the years of preparation it took to become a teacher, the average educator was unhappy enough to switch careers mid-stream. When teachers were asked why they were leaving, the most common response was, 'Everywhere I go in my profession there are too many people in the same place at the same time with too much to do and too little time to do it. I find it depressing to watch young people slip away for lack of the few minutes of attention and encouragement I never seem to be able to get around to giving them.' The system was rife with stereo-typical assumptions: for example, that all ten-year-olds would be ready for the same thing on the same day and could be tested and evaluated abased on their responses. There was simply no provision for and no appreciation of individual differences."

I felt so strongly about Glenn's material, I earned my master's degree so I could teach his course. I completed my degree driving two hours to Kearney Nebraska in the evenings, participating in a three-hour class, and then driving another two hours home. I was truly motivated.

I loved graduate school and felt I was really learning things I enjoyed and that were relevant to life. I received the opportunity to be a graduate assistant which helped pay for my degree. Katie, Drew, and I moved to Kearney my final year to finish, commuting back to our home in McCook on weekends.

During this time, I felt I was learning things that I should have been taught in my previous education experiences. Educational Psychology did not offer the comprehensive training I needed to understand my students' emotional needs. I was, for the first time, exposed to real-life learning about the social/emotional self.

My small high school had not offered psychology. My favorite course in high school had been sociology. I loved studying about cultures and human behavior. I would have loved the opportunity to break out of a system where math and science made me feel unintelligent and been able to study an area of interest.

I took a course when I was an undergraduate in college called Human Behavior Analysis and was instructed by the late John Glover. I was one of the only undergraduates in this class as most of the students were taking it as a graduate course and to me seemed "old." Of course, now those in their forties seem young to me!

I remember the stress my classmates felt completing the essay exams that consisted of example situations where we had to analyze human behaviors and defend our analysis. It was one of the few times in my life I felt smart. I still do not understand algebra, but I breezed through this course. It would be the only time in my life when a teacher pointed out my strengths. Along with an A+ in the top corner of my exam was a note written in the margin by Dr. Glover: "Well done! You should consider graduate school in this area."

I couldn't believe it! It was at that moment I became a better teacher. Even though I hadn't earned my degree, I had just experienced the importance and significance of helping students find their strengths.

This is why I embrace the work of Howard Gardner, Harvard professor, whose Theory of Multiple Intelligences explained so much to me about my own life. Over the years, I've used his work to educate students and parents. His theory helps to expand our thinking about what "smart" really is and that it doesn't just apply to academic core classes. Educational institutions focus on students' weak core academic areas. We then put all the emphasis on giving students extra direct instruction in those areas despite the misery created by being constantly faced with what you are "not" good at doing. It would be much more beneficial to work on weak areas through an area of strength. However, this requires more time, effort, and creativity, all rare commodities in today's educational environments.

I will never forget attending a conference called *Learning and The Brain* at Harvard University the first week of May in 1996, just a few short weeks after the horrific Columbine High School shootings. One of the breakout sessions I attended as a new school counselor was entitled "How Emotions Affect Learning." Of course, I wanted to attend this session to gain knowledge on this important issue. The presenter was rambling on about the amigdalya, the center of emotions, with a bunch of other technical information that was over the heads of most in the audience. We wanted him to bring it down to our level and tell us something useful about real-life situations. Then came the question/answer segment.

> "I have this theory that if one person can go out of their way to show compassion, then it will start a chain reaction of the same. People will never know how far a little kindness can go."
>
> -Rachel Scott, Rachel's Challenge (Rachel was the first victim in the Columbine shootings)

I was sitting in a large tiered auditorium towards the top when a woman sitting in the middle raised her hand and stifled the audience with her question: "I'm from Columbine High School; what do we do?"

Everyone leaned forward in their seat at the same time. We all wanted to know: how in the world do you come back after a massacre in your school and function on basic levels, much less learn? As a nation we were all still reeling from the tragic event. Knowing that someone from Columbine high school was in the audience instantly humbled the participants into utter silence as we waited for the answer.

I give the presenter credit for not trying to put together an answer; he simply admitted he did not know. He was a researcher working in a lab. Thus, the point: we may learn all kinds of things in college and workshops, but often it is real life that stumps us. This explains why we often lose ourselves teaching curriculums demanded of us, and neglect application to the real world.

The boys involved in the Columbine shootings were labeled "gifted" students, which meant they were very intelligent in one or more areas that schools assess for giftedness. Clearly poor academic skills were not the issue.

Two weeks before the Columbine shootings, William Pollack, author of the book, *Real Boys*, appeared on the Oprah Winfrey show. He outlined his Harvard Medical School research on boys. He explained how boys hide behind "masks," unable to understand or express their true feelings. As he explained further details including the very serious consequences that can result from this situation, he unknowingly was predicting the Columbine shootings. Sadly his work was affirmed in this real-life tragedy. Oprah Winfrey re-aired the show a few weeks after the shootings highlighting his chilling prediction and dire need for society to pay attention to his work.

There are no high-stakes tests for emotional intelligence. It really boils down to one question: how well does the individual understand and act upon his/her emotions? First one must recognize the emotion being experienced. Then insight is required to realize how behaviors affect emotions. Those who have chosen to stuff their feelings over the years are oblivious to the far-reaching effects this has on their behaviors and ability to have meaningful, lasting relationships.

Teaching about feelings is difficult! I use "feeling rocks," an idea presented in a workshop I attended while in graduate school. I created a lesson when I was an elementary school counselor and have found that it works for all ages in helping to understand that which is so elusive to us. I recently started doing lessons in my high school for our Relationships Class. I drag my rolling suitcase into school loaded with all different sized rocks that have various faces Katie and Drew painted on them years ago. I also bring Drew's old book bag as another lesson aid.

We begin with the simple question: "What is a feeling? Have you ever tried to define it?" It is anything but concrete! The dictionary definition states:

Definition of FEELING

....emotional state or reaction <a kindly *feeling* toward the boy> b *plural* : susceptibility to impression : ...<the remark hurt her *feelings*> 3a : the undifferentiated background of one's awareness considered apart from any identifiable sensation, perception, or thought b : the overall quality of one's awareness c : conscious recognition :.... 4a : often unreasoned opinion or belief :......5: capacity to respond emotionally especially with the higher emotions 6: the character ascribed to something :......7a : the quality of a work of art that conveys the emotion of the artist b : sympathetic aesthetic response

Wading through the dictionary definitions is difficult. What does it all really mean? This is when I refer to the feeling rocks. They are tangible and easily held throughout our discussion.

First, we notice the various sizes of the stones—some are small pebbles and others are large stones. We then relate the size of the rocks to the size of our emotions. Sometimes our emotions are less significant to our overall well-being while at other times, they consume us.

Next, we toss a few pebbles into the book bag. The pebbles represent lesser emotions and are easy to carry and do little to hinder movement. Then we examine the rocks that Drew and Katie painted faces on. Each represents a different emotion such as happiness, loneliness, anger, and sadness. As we load the bag with the larger rocks, we notice that the weight becomes burdensome. Then, as we completely stuff the bag with all sizes of rocks, daily functions become a challenge.

I ask the students to give examples of life experiences that represent the larger stones. Death and divorce are the most common responses. We also discuss that individual perception influences the emotional impact of most situations. Something that seems insignificant to one person may be overwhelming to another.

Finally, I have a student volunteer hoist the loaded bag on his shoul-

"Talking about feelings is of particular benefit as we engage thought and reasoning processes to comprehend and verbalize the emotional experience. This helps to strengthen the important emotion-cognition link.

...If they remain suppressed, denied, they precipitate a chronic release of adrenalin and depress learning, memory and immunity."

-Carla Hannaford, Smart Moves

ders and attempt to do daily tasks. I have the volunteer sit at a desk to do homework and then lie down to "sleep." Though comical, this awkward demonstration brings home the point. Emotions affect everything we do, and "stuffing" them causes tremendous stress on the mind and the body. We observe that the stuffed bag's seams are strained, indicating that when we are stressed, our physical well-being is also compromised. We then discuss coping strategies for dealing with powerful emotions and stress. We generate lists of good vs. bad methods of handling feelings and thoroughly examine the benefits and detriments of each approach.

When I was an elementary counselor, I always began my guidance curriculum with the rock lesson, and all other lessons were built around it. In every lesson, I would hold up the angry rock and ask students if it was okay to have that feeling. They would invariably say, "No."

I then explain that all feelings, even anger, are okay. However, anger often results in negative behavior if not managed properly. Amazingly, adults often answer this question in the same way. It is what we do with our feelings that can be positive or negative. It seems so simple, but we don't emphasize this enough. Even my attempts at providing useful guidance curriculum as an elementary counselor weren't nearly enough to effectively reach children and ensure sustained learning.

"Common sense is in spite of, not the result of, education."

-Victor Hugo

If social/emotional skills were integrated into all curriculum taught at every educational institution, we could make a dent in the deficits. Throughout the years, I've listened to the arguments that denigrate the D.A.R.E. (Drug Abuse Resistance Education)

The Children Left Behind

Prevention Program. Whether or not D.A.R.E was an effective program worth the investment, it is gone from the schools I've worked in and has been replaced with nothing.

If we exposed students to writing skills one time in fifth grade and found this to be ineffective, would we stop teaching it? Every year we graduate students lacking in basic academic skills reflecting years of ineffective programs, but we don't throw out all the academic programs. Instead we spend more time, money, and energy trying to teach the students more effectively.

> ***Perhaps keeping students off drugs and alcohol would remedy both problems.***

The media will greatly emphasize stories concerning events such as natural disasters, plane crashes, or contagious outbreaks of diseases, all which take many lives at once, but there is little said concerning the epidemic of drug and alcohol abuse. We've seen the fleeting stories of Hollywood celebrities who have died far too young, and even those stories do not lead us into action. Addiction is like a tornado. It has the power to kill and create havoc on everything in its path, and it destroys many relationships along the way. This is the untold story. Emotional intelligence is lost by the power and intensity of addiction. If we covered the stories of all who die each day to addiction, perhaps the appropriate level of attention would be given to this heartbreaking story as well.

- 14 -
Moving To Virginia
Land of The SOLS
(Standards of Learning)

Armed with my master's degree in education as we moved to Virginia, I hoped to teach "Developing Capable People" there. I quickly discovered that no one cared that I had found something so useful and wanted to share it with others. The state was ramping up with the Standards of Learning school reform. I was told I would never get my class approved unless it had SOL in the title.

The state was required to demonstrate compliance with the No Child Left Behind Act. It was in full swing with states developing high-stakes tests around standard- based learning. The reform movement took the existing gap and created a giant sink hole for many students who were sadly left behind before they even got to school.

I hadn't planned to use my counseling degree to work in schools. I was more interested in educational consulting, but after selling everything in Nebraska, our dental office deal fell through in Virginia. We moved anyway, and decided to figure it out when we got there. We purchased a small practice to get started and would later expand it.

While registering my son for kindergarten, the school counselor told me that she knew the county north of us needed an elementary counselor for a six-week maternity leave. She said that they had given up on finding someone and told the teachers they would be without their classroom Guidance.

As I previously mentioned, elementary teachers get few breaks and have many preps, so this type of news is never welcomed. Since we really needed the money, I did the six-week substitute position. The principal waited to introduce me at a staff meeting, announcing they would have Guidance after all. A rousing round of applause was a great way to start a job!

The next six weeks were a blur; consequently, I only remember a few details from my short time there. One was how overwhelming bus duty was. I couldn't figure out why the teachers had walkie talkies. Bus duty was definitely a new experience! It took over an hour to get all the students on busses and on their way home. Then I realized that all six hundred K-2 primary students were bussed to school.

I remember a young female student who became so frightened when she realized her father was at school, she hid under the teacher's desk. The teacher explained to me that she had witnessed her dad snapping her kitten's neck; she had good reason to be afraid of this man.

This short substituting stint introduced me to school counseling and its vital role in supporting both students and teachers.

While there, another county counselor informed me that the current governor had supported legislation requiring schools to choose between having a counselor or a reading specialist. I couldn't believe it. Who would imagine those positions to be even remotely close to serving the same needs for students? I'm not sure what a reading specialist could do for a child screaming under a desk in fear of her abusive father. Many of these situations are even beyond the scope of the school counselor's role, but families often do not make referrals to community agencies. This leaves the school counselor offering as much support as possible.

A few years later, I took a job as a part-time counselor in an elementary school in my county. I worked with fourth and fifth grade students. After an eight-year hiatus from education, I was soon to meet more children left behind in the schools where I would work.

- 15 -

Matthew

It was while writing this book that I remembered Matthew. My computer had gotten a virus and while waiting for its repair, I got on my old computer and searched for documents from the night class I eventually taught in Virginia. Despite not having Standards of Learning in the title, I was fortunate to have connections through my brother with the Director of the SW Virginia Higher Education Center. The Director helped me to organize a conference entitled "Creating Safe Schools," and we invited Stephen Glenn, creator of the "Developing Capable People" course, as our keynote speaker.

The University of Virginia's College at Wise then hired me as an adjunct instructor to teach a three-credit hour graduate course. The first night class was filled with participants from the conference. Each semester I created a power point highlighting real life reasons we must teach emotional intelligence. The slides quoted students during my first years as a school counselor, leaving out names to protect their anonymity. I found one of those power point presentations while searching my old computer. The quotes in the beginning of this book were taken from that power point presentation.

How could I have forgotten Matthew's story? There were his words on my computer, each slide telling just a snippet of his horrific story. It was then I remembered his father talking to me about why he was having so many problems in school. His dad also had a rough upbringing and said he'd been beaten as a child and wore long sleeve shirts to cover the bruises. But, as he explained, it was nothing compared to what his son, Matthew, had endured. Matthew was a fifth grade boy, often distracted, who had been living with his mom and stepfather. After Matthew's biological father spoke with me, I had assured him I would see Matthew throughout the remaining year to offer support.

"Whereas a girl might share her feelings as soon as she's asked what's going wrong, a boy will often refuse (or ignore us) the first time he's approached."

-William Pollack, Ph.D., Real Boys

Matthew actually opened up more quickly than most boys. I explained to Matthew that his father had described what had happened with his stepfather, and I asked if he wanted to talk about the incident. He replied, "I'm just trying to get over it." He went on to say that his stepdad had been very agitated that night, and then he took a gun and just did it.

Matthew's stepfather had shot himself in the head in front of both Matthew and his mother. He offered the details of blood and brain parts

104

flying everywhere. Here was a young boy telling me that his mom needed counseling because she still had the brain-splattered glasses belonging to her deceased husband. Matthew's father was right; no child should have to witness such a terrible thing.

His test scores did not matter to him. Closing his eyes at night and attempting to erase the terrifying images were what mattered.

This was terrifying and overwhelming to me, and I was only listening to the story. The support this young boy needed was no less than our soldiers need when returning home from a war zone. In both situations the support is usually minimal, despite the devastation created by Post Traumatic Stress Disorder. Mental/emotional health issues are simply not a priority in our society. I worked two-and-a-half days per week since I was only half-time. This school could have used two full-time counselors, and still there would have been students with unmet needs.

Matthew

- 16 -

Susan

While at home on my day off, my colleague and dear friend called to report what had happened with Susan, one of my fourth grade students. Social Services had been called to the school. My friend retrieved Susan from the classroom so they could speak to her in the counseling office. Susan described the rage her mom had unleashed on her the night before. This was corroborated with a trip to the nurse's office where the imprint of the board on her bottom was still visible. Susan said she counted each hit but stopped keeping track in the twenties. Learning the state standards is not important to a child who is beaten so severely she can barely sit down.

My colleague, who had many years of experience, was clearly shaken on the phone as she recounted this trying day. I was heartsick that I was not there for my student. But, the priority was not spending money on counseling departments. Counselors don't drill facts into students' heads.

Therefore, we were considered "nonessential" to those who created reform budgets.

Later, the family's dysfunction would rear its ugly head even further. The only consequence for Susan's beating was court-ordered counseling. No one checked to see if the mother had complied. Susan acted out the following year. She had been ostracized by her family, which is common in these situations. She injured her sister's arm with a screw driver, and the mom was more than pleased to prove to the Department of Social Services that the problems in this family were Susan's fault. In addition, the mother insisted Susan should pay for her actions.

I recall her mom emphasizing to our principal how badly Susan's behavior had been toward her sister. As I listened, it took every ounce of restraint to refrain from commenting. Despite what had just happened, I knew the truth regarding the cruelty in this home and the lack of assistance from Social Services when Susan was so badly beaten by her mother. I went immediately to my office and called the caseworker to inquire how it could be that the original victim in this situation was now regarded as the guilty one.

So many times over the years I witnessed the system failing these

> "It is with great pleasure and deep personal and emotional satisfaction that I have had the opportunity to see Dave rise above his excruciating childhood. He is a living example and a model to others who have suffered under similar circumstances. As Dave walked out of juvenile hall in 1974, as a child, I bade him good luck. And as he walked back into juvenile hall in 1989, as a counselor, I felt a tear in my eye and simply said, 'Bravo.'"
>
> -Dave Pelzer, *The Lost Boy*

children. Susan's case had been labeled "unfounded" despite the physical evidence to prove otherwise. A total lack of acknowledgement there had been a crime was the implication. To me, this is a crime in and of itself, especially when it involves a defenseless child. In Susan's case, I feel certain she was left completely unacknowledged. In my opinion, we should always error on the side of the child until there is proof otherwise.

Again, there was not enough money for more caseworkers who would have time to investigate and follow up on these crimes. However, there was plenty of money to pay testing companies. In fact, the report on how much the state was spending on testing was kept quiet when the governor was up for re-election. I never saw the report but would later hear from a local School Board member that is was an enormous amount of money.

Susan

- 17 -
Priorities

As I write, I feel my heart pounding. I relive the awful moments sitting with children who had been abused and attempting to assure them the system would protect them, knowing this probably wasn't true. How can it be that our innocent children are not protected? This continues to be a consuming frustration.

The year my colleague was harshly scrutinized by the state after standardized test administrations further emphasized the financial priority placed on testing. I was thankful that I was only assisting with the testing. The amount of time and money invested in the test procedures themselves was beyond ridiculous. I specifically recall the amount of time it took me to read and comprehend the explicit instructions for packing the boxes to return the tests to the state. I was resentful that I was expected to dedicate my time to something that had nothing to do with providing counseling services to our students.

That year, my colleague received a letter from the state stating that when the test prompts for the writing tests were received, one was missing from our boxes. We had, however, not indicated any were missing when we did our final counts and packed the boxes. These boxes were then transferred to our district offices and recounted by district personnel and finally sent on to the state.

We will never know where that prompt was lost or who failed to count correctly, but what we did know was the procedure cost an incredible amount of time and money. We also knew who the state was blaming for the error. To this day, I wish I had asked for a copy of the letter. As my friend read it to me, I again thought, How has our country come to this? The prevalence of government control and now, fear tactics, simply did not feel American.

"The single best way to produce creativity is freedom. The power to decide what to do and how to do it...a sense of control over one's own ideas and work. Among things that smother creativity are frequent evaluation and criticism. Those most inhibited in creativity are those who are in high pressure environments."

-Anonymous

This letter stated that the entire state testing system had been compromised because of the negligence in handling these materials. To add further insult to the situation, once the tests reached the state for scoring, individuals with no qualifications were hired to evaluate the writing tests. Two readers for each test—that was how our tax dollars were being spent. The state would advertise for these positions, provide some training, and then dole out every fifth and eleventh grade writing test from the entire state to these individuals to assess. Each test was evaluated by two readers.

It is unimaginable that we don't trust our teachers to design and grade their own tests. I know how to read and write, thanks to my small town high school teachers who created and graded tests without government help. Government control at this level does nothing to weed out the bad teachers. It will, however, weed out the good ones. But what is most disheartening is that all of this money could be used far more effectively to address the mental health issues of our children.

> "Intelligence plus character-that is the goal of true education."
>
> -Martin Luther King Jr.

A few years later, after moving to Colorado, I turned on the television and discovered there had been a shooting at Virginia Tech. I called Katie's friend, a student at Virginia Tech, to check on her. She said things were fine on campus and that she was okay. Many of Katie's high school classmates were then juniors at Tech. In addition, many of my former middle school students were on campus, expanding my worries.

I had barely gotten off the phone with Katie's friend when the media report revealed that over a dozen were dead. I couldn't breathe. Tears filled my eyes as I called my daughter. We tried to make sense of what was happening. I spent the day glued to the television watching this madness unfold. It would be around four in the afternoon when I received a call from my good friend in Virginia informing me that all of our students were unharmed. Yet, thirty-two innocent students were dead.

When I imagine the ringing of unanswered cell phones as bodies encased in bags were removed from the building, my heart still breaks.

*How the students who died that day scored on their SOL tests and SAT
scores for admission to Virginia Tech did not matter.
How much the shooter needed mental health care
did matter. But those in power did not heed the warnings.*

It took thirty-two dead for the discussion to be focused on mental health in the state of Virginia. Why did it take thirty two deaths to finally have the conversation that so many tried to initiate with legislators over the years? I spent the day wringing my hands and again thinking about school shootings and the lack of emotional intelligence curriculum. We had not learned from Columbine and having spent ten frustrating years in Virginia, and witnessing the amount of money spent testing, I wanted to call the governor myself and discuss the serious spending deficit on mental health issues. I wanted to tell him about Matthew and Susan and about an innocent little girl who saw her kitten's neck broken at the hands of her abusive father. I wanted to ask him to please look at the enormous amount of money his state was spending on administering tests while these children suffered.

Time, money, and many resources were spent investigating the Virginia Tech shooting only to arrive at similar conclusions. While Virginia Tech was headlines across the world, my students' stories were left untold.

- 18 -

Rushing Children and Giving Points

During my last year of counseling at the Virginia elementary school, one of our veteran first grade teachers was retiring. I told her what a loss to education her retirement would be. She replied she could no longer teach with the new SOL system. She did not believe in giving points to teach reading as was required by the prescribed Accelerated Reading Program. She further felt that young children were required to learn skills they were not developmentally ready to master.

The knowledge I had gained over the years reading authors such as Jane Healy in *Endangered Minds* and Alfie Kohn in *Punished By Rewards*, and

> "There can be no happiness if what we do is different than what we believe."
>
> -Dr. Kent Estes

115

The Schools Our Children Deserve, confirmed her viewpoint. The content in each of these books validated the wisdom of her words. If only someone would explain these premises to policy makers who pass developmentally inappropriate requirements. There are both biological as well as psychological consequences when this occurs.

Healy's explanation regarding the biological reasons we should not rush children into learning skills beyond their developmental level is compelling. She carefully outlines how human brain systems develop myelin which aids in transmission as they grow and mature. This process begins in childhood and moves from the brain's lower to higher-level systems. Healy states that "myelination of the brain" is not complete until individuals are in their twenties and beyond. She warns, "Before brain regions are myelinated, they do not operate efficiently. For this reason, trying to 'make' children master academic skills for which they do not have the requisite maturation may result in mixed-up patterns of learning."

She uses the teaching of algebra as one example which is interesting to note given the current trend to push Algebra I and Algebra II into late middle school and the first years of high school. Healy refers to her own personal confusion when learning equations using X, Y, and Z and how she, and many others she has spoken with over the years, avoided math courses because of this bewilderment. She discusses how later in life many are "forced" into math courses in graduate schools where they suddenly discover their brains have matured with the reasoning skills needed in understanding higher level complex math. Healy states, "The areas to receive the last dose of myelin are the association areas responsible for manipulating highly abstract concepts—such as symbols (X, Y, Z; graphs) that stand for other symbols (numerical relationships) that stand for real things."

On a regular basis I have witnessed Healy's observations: "....children decide they are 'dumb' about certain subjects, when the truth is that someone simply laid on the learning too soon in a form other than the one they needed to receive it in at the time."

When I'm expected to schedule a student in the same algebra class three years in a row because they have yet to master the subject, I have no doubt there are painful psychological consequences.

Unfortunately, the educational reform story gets worse as the most recent common core standards require even more difficult math courses for young high school students with no acknowledgement or flexibility for individual differences in development. *Endangered Minds* was written in 1990 by Healy, acclaimed Colorado author and educator. It is very clear that policymakers have never read her insightful words: "Since every child's developmental schedule may be different for every type of learning (e.g., some get better at math faster than at English and vice versa), this concept of plasticity makes teaching a challenging task indeed."

We continue to try to reform education on the premise that "standardization" and "common core" curriculum can produce learners who master the same learning objectives at the same time in the same way.

I would like to know if there is anyone who can go out into his or her garden and "make" every flower bloom at the exact same time and further ensure that each bloom is equally large and beautiful. It defies nature; so why do we expect all students to master the same content, taught in the same way, on the same day? Making this expectation even more ridiculous would be if some of the flowers were planted in poor soul, without proper nutrients and water, and void of any care, while others were planted in fertile soils, watered, and given plenty of attention and care.

E.D. Hirsch, who has written numerous books on the subject of education and what students should know, as outlined in his "core knowledge" philosophy, would not agree with me on this matter. His "core knowledge" program was adopted as the foundation of the Standards Of Learning reform that the state of Virginia incorporated to improve education.

However, even Dr. Hirsch, when answering a question from members of my night class during a speaking engagement, did agree that "core knowledge" should not be ALL that is taught. The class asked him about teaching social/emotional skills to students. He replied that "core knowledge" should comprise only fifty percent of the curriculum so there was adequate time for other important curriculum. He further acknowledged having no control over what the state of Virginia had done in regards to the standards they adopted for their reform movement.

When Drew was in first grade, he came home one night upset because at lunch he had to sit at a table with a few other students away from the reading party table where students were treated to pizza for earnings reading points. I was so upset for my son. We had purposely not entered the contest because I believe, as Kohn points out in his book *Punished By Rewards*, that we create selfish individuals when a reward of some kind is attached to every accomplishment. This practice destroys intrinsic motivation.

Kohn highlights the same philosophy that the retiring teacher had expressed to me when she said she did not believe in giving points as a way to teach reading. This excerpt from the back cover summary of Kohn's book describes his arguments against bribery in schools: "Alfie Kohn shows that while manipulating people with incentives seems to work in the short run, it is a strategy that ultimately fails and even does lasting harm. Drawing from hundreds of studies, Kohn demonstrates that people actually do inferior work when they are enticed with money, grades, or other incentives. The more we use artificial inducements to motivate people, the more they lose interest in what we're bribing them to do."

For the same reasons, I did not have any across-the-board rewards as a young teacher. Our point chart reflected only a random sample of students' on-task behaviors. Before I had even read Kohn's work, I inherently knew the goal should be to learn for the sake of learning, not for a reward every time. My own observations in the classroom reiterated Kohn's argument that when rewards are attached to productivity, work ethic actually diminishes.

Now, here was my son broken-hearted because he had been ostracized at lunch. He was insightful even as a young child, though, and quickly rebounded, commenting that he didn't care about the pizza; he just liked to read. Kohn's idea to reward a child for reading by giving them another book was exemplified in this situation.

We decided to have our own celebration, and we each found a favorite book that evening and curled up together in a large, comfy chair to read. I knew then that our move to Virginia was going to be a challenge for my children's education since the teaching methods often contradicted what I strongly believed.

During this same year, I took Drew to visit a museum in Richmond,

Virginia which featured the roaming exhibit, *The Hundred Languages of Children* by students in Regio Emilia, Italy. I had seen the display with a fellow teacher the week before. The exhibits and workshops being offered were on early childhood education.

My friend and I entered the museum where we saw the most amazing displays of work. I saw a giant giraffe made of plastic milk cartons and shoe boxes, self portraits that looked like the work of middle school students, and intricate maps of a city's water system. I said, "We must be wrong place because I thought the oldest 'artists' were just six years old."

My friend started reading the tags under the artwork. The self portraits were five and six-year-olds; other works were produced by students even younger. It was unbelievable.

We were utterly amazed and highly motivated to return the next week to hear Lillian Katz, a guru in early childhood education. In her article written with Dianne McClellan entitled *Young Children's Social Development: A Checklist*, they write, "Indeed, the single best childhood predictor of adult adaptation in not IQ, not school grades, and not classroom behavior but, rather the adequacy with which the child gets along with other children. Children who are generally disliked, who are aggressive and disruptive, who are unable to sustain close relationships with other children, and who cannot establish a place for themselves in the peer culture are seriously 'at risk'. (Hartup, 1992). The risks are many: poor mental health, dropping out of school, low achievement and other school difficulties, poor employment history, and so forth (see Katz and McClellan, 1991). Given the life-long consequences, relationships should be counted as the first of the four R's of education."

I wanted Drew to see this exhibit. There were light tables with beads and a triangular shaped mirror a person could crawl into and see endless reflections of themselves. I knew Drew would love it.

When we returned that second week with him, he went straight to the light table and started playing with the beads but quickly stopped, looked up at me, and asked, "What are we supposed to do?"

I glanced at my friend and said, "That response is the product of American education."

We are so full of directions and coloring in the box that by first grade, Drew asked for the directions. His natural instincts and development attracted him to the table, but he was only there a few minutes before asking me for instructions.

My daughter's graduating class of 2004 would be the first impacted by the state's Standards of Learning Reform movement. She was in fifth grade when we moved to Virginia, and it eventually became obvious that she had been subjected to SOLs when any situation arose that required some thought. She would ask me a question and I would say, "Let's think about that."

She would interrupt me and reply, "Just tell me the answer."

She is a bright, talented young woman, and it is upsetting when I realize the void in opportunities for independent thinking her Virginia education offered. Luckily, both she and Drew attended small private liberal arts colleges where they were exposed to learning that required critical thinking versus memorization.

That last year working as an elementary counselor in Virginia brought the life-changing decision to end my marriage. It was heart-wrenching and will always be one of the biggest disappointments of my life. However, I had learned to accept the things in life I could not change.

Forging ahead meant finding a full-time job so I could support myself. There was an opening in our local middle school where Drew would attend the following year. I was very relieved when the job was offered to me. It would be comforting to be at the same school with Drew and just across the street from Katie's high school during this tumultuous time in our lives.

Since I had been working with fourth and fifth grade students, moving to middle school seemed a natural transition. I knew that I would either love this age or hate it. There didn't seem to be any in-between when talking with fellow educators.

I did love this age, despite all the drama from raging hormones and altering brains and bodies! As in my previous job, I was surprised at what my students were exposed to at such young ages. It was not at all like my junior high years. If students were engaging in oral sex on a regular basis back then, I surely didn't know about it.

Sex, drugs, alcohol use, and the "gay" drama were all prevalent issues I was confronted with on a regular basis as a middle school counselor. I attribute much of this to television and movies. I know that these issues have always existed, but nothing like we see today. As many have said before me, if companies can spend millions of dollars for a thirty-second advertisement during the Super Bowl, then obviously what we see on television DOES affect our behaviors.

- 19 -
Valerie

Valerie was not the type of student to ever step foot into a counseling office. She was a strong-willed, in-your-face seventh grade student. She had an older brother who had begun high school her seventh grade year; it would be that year she would start to carve on herself.

"Cutters" were usually girls who took sharp objects and made cuts on various places on their bodies. Typically, the arms were where I would see evidence of the "cutting." "Cutting" is a ritual that is used by some as a coping mechanism. Students explained the physical pain from "cutting" helped them to forget about their emotional pain. Valerie was definitely trying to escape her emotional pain by "cutting." It took a friend escorting her to my office to convince her that talking with me was a better option.

There were many "cutters" I worked with in my four years at the middle school. Again, there was an undeniable need for curriculum to address these issues, but it wasn't one of the state's standards. Very little time was given for classroom guidance, and then it centered on career counseling, not emotional issues.

"Therapy can teach girls to identify early that they are in pain. They need to label their internal state as painful and then think about how to proceed. They must learn new ways to deal with intense misery and also new ways to process pain. Their stock way has been to hurt themselves."

-Mary Piper, Ph.D., Reviving Ophelia

The first few times I had Valerie in to talk, she didn't. She stubbornly refused to engage in any conversation pertaining to her feelings. We could discuss the weather, how she liked her civics class, etc., but that was it. I informed her mom that she was "cutting" and referred her for outside services. This was ignored until finally I phoned enough times to warrant a call to Social Services for medical neglect. Mandated counseling resulted from the call.

Valerie eventually began to trust me enough to talk a little, but mostly she just looked at me with eyes reflecting the painful secrets she couldn't yet verbalize. She knew that I suspected there was something very significant she needed to tell me.

Months later, with her friend by her side, she told me what she had already told her friends: her brother had sexually assaulted her. The confusion regarding her love for her brother and the assault were apparent, and the family's unspoken secret rules, very clear.

Luckily, an outside counselor was already in place. Now came the hard part—hoping the call to Social Services would be beneficial rather than harmful to Valerie. I was upfront with her as I explained the process, and that she would need to tell what happened again to someone unfamiliar.

In this county in Virginia, the intake worker who took reports at the Social Services office had the inappropriate habit of "trying" the case while the report was being made and often concluded that nothing could be done. It was good I never met the man in person. We were in the trenches with children who needed help, and he seemed like the enemy rather than an ally. When you are on my end of the phone line, you do not care how overloaded caseworkers are at Social Services. You, too, are overloaded and must look into the eyes of a child in pain hoping the system will work.

When I made the initial report, he told me there was nothing Social Services could do because the brother was a family member and not a caregiver to his sister.

I replied angrily, "Are you kidding me? Your agency is called Child Protection Services!" I informed him that her family had ignored the fact that she was "cutting" herself and had to be mandated to get her help, and now she was molested by a sibling while in their care; therefore this was under their jurisdiction.

He decided to take my report. I then discovered a male social worker had been assigned to the case. Valerie was at a difficult age and in a horrific situation; I felt it would have been easier for her to express herself with a female caseworker. The interview took place in my office. As predicted, Valerie was reluctant to open up to the male caseworker; consequently, the interview was lengthy.

She was not removed from the home because her brother left to live with an older sibling.

A few weeks later on a Friday night, I received a call on my cell phone from Valerie. I have given my personal number on only a couple occasions

> "Because I am not worthy enough to be a member of 'The Family,' I lie on top of an old, worn-out army cot without a blanket."
>
> -Dave Pelzer, *A Man Named Dave*

over the years, but felt strongly she may need it if things got out of control, especially given her reluctance to talk to strangers.

Things were not going well at home. The family had disowned her, and on that particular evening, she was left alone as the rest of the family gathered up the road at another family member's home for a party. They made it very clear to Valerie she was not a part of the family anymore. Overwhelmed with emotion, she could not handle this rejection.

While talking with her on the phone that evening, she told me that she had already knocked several holes in the walls of her room. I told her to take some deep breaths while I contacted Social Services. Thankfully, the caseworker came to her aid and she was placed in a foster home. She could now seek the respite she needed from the chaos and dysfunction of her home and find care and concern from her foster family.

Her recovery was going to be long and painful and I'm certain is still ongoing today.

Valerie was a bright young girl; however this could not possibly be reflected on her State tests. Tests do not matter when your family has betrayed you.

– 20 –
An Unexpected Chapter

It was July, 2012, and Drew was home from college for a few weeks as I was writing these chapters. I got up early the morning of July twentieth to prepare for a walk with a friend. The night before, Drew and I had decided at the last minute to go see a movie. We attended a six o'clock show and noticed a line of campers out front waiting to get tickets for the opening midnight showing of *The Dark Knight Rises*.

That morning I turned on the television as I pulled on my sneakers for walking. On the screen I saw **Breaking News: Mass Shooting**, scrolling across the bottom. I stopped and listened.

As with the Oklahoma City bombing, Columbine High School, Virginia Tech, and 9/11, my heart pounded and a lump formed in my throat. Twelve were dead and over fifty wounded following a mass shooting at a theater in Aurora, Colorado. Innocent movie goers had gathered for a midnight showing of *The Dark Knight Rises*. Now they were victims of another senseless shooting.

The summer of 2012 also saw raging fires across the state of Colorado that caused massive destruction of property and natural resources. However, the fires were, for the most part, an act of nature. The theater shooting was the act of a man. Again, we pondered the question, *Why? What kind of person commits such a horrendous crime?*

A text came from a coworker: "What is happening to our State?"

Someone posts on Facebook: "Forget about gun control; when are we going to talk about mental health?"

YES! When are we going to have that discussion? And when are we going to pay attention to the effects of viewing violence?

I have a two-inch stack of articles that I downloaded some years ago from the American Pediatric Society's website. We pay attention when warned about childhood illness, yet we ignore warnings about viewing violence. Ironically, some of the midnight viewers of the *The Dark Knight Rises* thought the gunshots they heard were part of the movie. *Why did many still want to attend this violent show?*

Later in the day as the sickening details unraveled, we discovered that James Holmes had been a Ph.D. student at the University of Colorado's Medical School. Obviously, a bright mind by academic standards, but clearly the emotional mind was unhealthy.

Another story. More questions. Here was an academic scholar in neuroscience, studying those with psychiatric illness. It was unbelievable.

Unfortunately, this chapter was added before I even finished this book. However, this incident stands to strengthen my point. We are all left behind when we do not realize that emotional health dictates the rest of the story. There has always been and there always will be mental illness, just as there will always be physical illness and disease. They are not separate entities. Each has far reaching effects on the other.

My hope is simply that we prioritize emotional intelligence in education so that we all have a better understanding of the issues that plague so many each and every day. Then perhaps we will recognize the warning signs in people like James Holmes before it's too late.

In memory of those who died in a theater in Colorado and in honor of the survivors of this tragedy, I dedicate this chapter.

An Unexpected Chapter

- 21 -
Natalie

I began working with Natalie when she was in seventh grade. I remember her grandmother coming in to register her for school because she had taken custody of Natalie and her younger sister. Natalie's mom was unable to care for the girls due to poor life choices which included multiple boyfriends, drinking, and drug abuse. I don't recall why I was out in the parking lot when the girls left with their grandmother that day, but I do remember Natalie's face as she waited for her grandmother to unlock the car doors. She looked extremely anxious.

Later, I would understand her facial expression. Natalie shared her feelings with greater ease than Valerie. I soon learned about the physical and emotional abuse that was occurring in her grandmother's home. Natalie also shared things with some of the teachers in our building. Social Services had been called on numerous occasions, yet Natalie was still in the home. In fact, things were worse because Grandma was furious that Natalie was talking at school. A frustration regarding reporting to Social Services is there is seldom any follow-up.

As repeated abuse occurred, Natalie became more upset with me. I told her I had to call Social Services, but she knew they weren't helping and feared continued retribution from her grandmother. The frustrations with systems put in place to assist children that fail was nearly unbearable. Social Services does not have any ongoing follow-up communication with schools once a report has been made to them. Similar scenes across America are regularly reported in the news.

I called and asked the assigned caseworker why they were not doing anything. She eventually admitted that she did not believe Natalie. Instead, she felt Natalie's mom had told her to lie about the living conditions with her grandmother in an effort to regain custody.

As the situation continued that year, several concerned teachers approached me because nothing was being done to help Natalie. When I relayed the message from the caseworker, they were as enraged as I had been. We decided to by-pass the caseworker and call the program director. I set up the meeting when all involved teachers could attend. There is power in numbers, and we desperately needed it in this situation.

None of us believed Natalie had made up the stories, and we felt our combined years of experience should be credible. The caseworker attended the meeting as well and gave her version of the actions she had and hadn't taken in the case of Natalie and her younger sister. The teachers each gave their versions of what Natalie had revealed to them and further, how her behaviors caused them to believe her.

The absurdity of this meeting is still clear today. We should not have needed to plead our young student's case. We should ALWAYS err on the side of safety for the child and then verify the facts. If that had been the case, Natalie would have been removed from her grandmother's care until facts were confirmed. Time and money were again our enemies, and this was exacerbated by the caseworker's lack of judgment and common sense. These are unnerving factors when considering the high stakes—the safety of a child.

Eventually, Natalie and her sister were removed. The situation filled me with anger. I wrote lawmakers and begged them to listen as I outlined situations where our systems were broken resulting in our children paying the price. I later met with our local state senator to plead for assistance. He listened and promised to help.

Since we moved to Colorado the following year, I don't know if our meeting made any difference. But again, no matter how bleak a situation seems, failure is not trying.

Natalie's story did not have a happy ending. She was truly failed by the system. A few years later, I asked some of my former coworkers about Natalie and was told she had run away and was found with a friend along the interstate. Shortly after, she got pregnant.

Natalie's teachers were held accountable for her
test scores regardless of her whereabouts.

The lack of emotional intelligence that trickled down through the generations was very apparent in this family. Valerie's grandmother had subjected her mother to abuse, and her mom, unequipped with coping mechanisms, began a life of addictions and poor choices. Natalie ended up in her grandmother's abusive home and the cycle continued. And now Natalie would introduce a new life into this dysfunctional cycle.

- 22 -
Alicia

I was called to the office to register a new seventh grade student. This would be the day I would meet Alicia, one of the most challenging students I have ever encountered. Alicia slouched in a corner chair of the main office. Her mom sat beside her. Alicia's make-up enhanced her black attire, and chains that hung from various pockets. I introduced myself and welcomed her to our middle school, which resulted in not one, but two eye rolls. I asked her what electives she might be interested in. She shrugged her shoulders.

Her mom interrupted. "I'm sorry, Mrs. Doty, that she talks and dresses like a thug. She was in a large school in Maryland where they had to go through metal detectors just to get in, and she acts like this because she had to there to protect herself. I keep telling her it's not that way here, and she doesn't need to act like that anymore."

Alicia again rolled her eyes. I acknowledged her mom's explanation and assured Alicia that our middle school was a safe place. She shrugged her shoulder and slouched further down in the chair.

I took her to the counseling office and began working on her schedule on the computer. These are the moments counselors dread—where to place a student such as Alicia? I reviewed each seventh grade teams' numbers and considered the teachers' personalities. She would be on the Blue team with two of my close friends.

When we finished the registration, I introduced her to the team. I saw the look on my two colleagues' faces as they assessed Alicia's attire and attitude which screamed, "I am mad at the world!"

On the teachers' first break they came to my office and expressed grave concerns. These are two of the finest teachers I've ever worked with, but they had never experienced anything quite like this. We were all very nervous about Alicia. She was mad, and that was something no one could miss when meeting her. What was most frightening was that she didn't have to say a word to convey this message.

After only a few days, there were reports of Alicia making threats to students. The teachers and I felt that this was worthy of suspension, but our principal did not agree. By the end of the second week, Drew and I overheard parents talking about "the new seventh grade student" at the annual PTA spaghetti supper. Word had spread quickly, and they were clearly afraid. Calls began pouring in as parents expressed their concerns to our principal.

Shortly after the PTA supper, the principal came into my office with Alicia in tow. Both were red-faced and clearly angry. My principal told me to talk with Alicia while he contacted the school resource officer. He was going to press charges for the threat that Alicia had made that day. He stomped out, clearly feeling the pressures of his position. Alicia had written this threat down. She was going to stab a boy in the carotid artery with a pencil outside the boys' bathroom at two o'clock. As Alicia fumed in front of me, I wished I didn't know these details. I was the only full-time counselor, and my office was far from the main office if things got out of hand.

I told Alicia to sit in the rocking chair, and I sat closest to the exit, just in case. When angry, Alicia had a vein that protruded in her temple. That day, the vein bulged and matched the color in her cheeks. I took a deep breath and asked Alicia to do the same.

Then I looked her into her eyes and said, "Alicia, you have one of the biggest chips on your shoulder of any student I have ever worked with. It is clear you are very angry, and what I know about anger is that it comes from hurt. So, what I'm wondering is, who has hurt you so much that you are this angry at the world?"

I held my breath expecting some choice expletives to be hurled my way. I also checked to see where my pencils were and was glad they were not within her reach! I will never forget what happened as my question sank in. It took her completely off-guard, and her entire demeanor relaxed from the bulging vein to her tense shoulders.

She thought for a brief moment, looked at me, and said, "Well, if you want me to tell you who has hurt me, then you will need to get your box of Kleenex over there because we are going to need it."

That was all it took to break her steely exterior. She began her story.

It would be well over an hour before the resource officer arrived to press charges, but Alicia was not finished with her story. Although I can't remember every detail, I do know it was laced with drugs, alcohol, domestic disputes, child abuse, and multiple suicides. In one of the domestic disputes, a sibling was thrown onto a glass table that shattered. Everywhere Alicia turned, adults were making poor choices and consuming drugs and alcohol regularly. She had been volleyed from her mom to her dad and back to her mom. Each had significant others in their lives with whom Alicia would try to bond. She described the suicide of two adults she had formed relationship with in the past few years. She explained how hard it was to get over the first death, and then she had to face another death. All this and she was only a young seventh grade child.

The principal and resource officer took her back to the main office even though she was far from finished revealing her lifelong heartache. She was suspended from school for a couple of weeks for the threats she had made.

Standards of Learning do not matter when you are simply trying to survive each hour of your life so filled with violence and chaos.

Now I was faced with the task of calming the entire seventh grade, including the staff. Since Alicia had begun tearing down her wall of anger and pain, I hoped we could now help her assimilate into her new school. I felt safer and more confident, and I hoped this would rub off on the others.

I called a team meeting with the two seventh grade classes that comprised her team. I spoke with the teachers before the meeting and described some of what had occurred in my office that day. I had asked Alicia for permission to share with the teachers and her classmates about the difficulties in her life. I promised her I would not tell details, but would simply ask them for understanding and compassion. She agreed to this, which gave me hope that when she returned, she would attempt to make friends with both the students and teachers. She needed care and support which was blatantly lacking in her home life.

Fifty students with their teachers solemnly waited for what I was about to say. There was no need to get their attention; you could have heard a pin drop. They knew we were going to discuss Alicia, and they were afraid and ready to listen.

I asked them to trust me, and assured them that I understood Alicia's threats were very frightening to all of us. I asked them if they could tell Alicia was very angry; they all readily nodded, yes. I then explained what I understood about anger, and that it often comes from being hurt. People use anger as a defense to ward off pain.

I told them that I had asked Alicia who had caused her so much pain. I described how Alicia's anger had dissipated as she began to describe the ways she had been hurt. I further explained that they did not need to know those private details; instead, they just simply needed to understand that her bad behavior came from her emotional pain, and she really needed friends.

We discussed how befriending someone who had exhibited such negative behavior was challenging. They were a kind, caring group of seventh graders willing to give Alicia another chance. As I talked, I removed myself from the group and stepped into a corner where I was alone. I explained that no one wants to be "out;" we all want to belong. Alicia's behaviors removed her from the team. She needed some hands to invite her back.

Again, I asked them to trust me. I assured them that they could come to their teachers or to me if they felt afraid for any reason. I sensed that they understood my message and would try to do as I requested. Then the students were allowed to ask questions and discuss the past two weeks with Alicia.

When given the opportunity to share and discuss, young people are amazingly insightful and willing to help make their schools better learning environments.

I recently had a perceptive discussion with one of my high school students about this subject, and I asked him if he would be willing to write down his thoughts about a retreat he had attended where students were given the opportunity to voice their opinions. Here is what he wrote: "Going on the Student Effectiveness Retreat had a major impact on my life, both academically and socially. I had the privilege of discussing my experiences with high school and my opinions about the processes by which the education system is run. I was given the chance to voice my opinions openly and comfortably with my peers, as well as with faculty members and even administration. The comfortable setting created through various activities and discussions allowed my peers and I to be completely honest and truthful without the fear of being rejected or made fun of.

"Once walls were torn down, I realized that I was not alone in a number of my opinions. I realized that my peers and I, though very unique and diverse, had more in common than expected. The discovery that I was not alone was one of the most liberating and shocking realizations in my life. In those three short days, inseparable bonds and unexpected friendships were created. The amount of learning was astounding. We discussed stereotypes and judgments and talked about how to break down the stereotypes. We talked about being different and diverse. It was amazing to me how much different the atmosphere was once everyone felt comfortable. People were more willing to discuss and voice their opinions, allowing others to learn from the different perspectives and opinions. Discussion flourished, and we, both students as well as staff members, were able to list issues and questions that we had about high school and what isn't working including the lack of a voice for students and the lack of deeper relationships between teachers and students."

> "When you take the time to actually listen, with humility, to what people have to say, it's amazing what you can learn. Especially if the people who are doing the talking also happen to be children."
>
> -Greg Mortenson,
> Stones Into Schools

From my first class meeting so many years ago in a small elementary school in Nebraska, to a middle school team meeting, to today in my current high school, the power of allowing time for **the forgotten education** is evident.

Alicia returned to school a few weeks later. I met with Alicia and her mom and shared the outcome of the classroom meeting. I explained that I had put myself on the line for her, and that I hoped she would take positive steps to try to make friends. It was clear her demeanor had changed. There was no anger on her face that day, so I was hopeful things would improve. It seemed that having the chance to share some of her pain had forged the path for bonds in her new school. If she wanted things to work, she would have to try to get along.

While the next months of school were not completely without incidents, it was a night-and-day improvement. Her classmates were caring and patient beyond our expectations. I still feel great pride in the teachers and students. They all showed amazing grace in a very frightening situation, and it paid off. I truly believe that different circumstances would have yielded a much different result.

The teachers and students created a relationship with Alicia, and that makes all the difference.

If only there had been a standard of learning for this; they would have aced that test.

For Alicia, her home life continued to be fraught with drug and alcohol abuse. I spent many hours over the following two years counseling Alicia. Transitioning to eighth grade was again difficult, though not as bad as her previous year. She now had no team, but instead, a different teacher each period of the day. She was not equipped to deal with that, and still needed a team as her "place to belong."

One day she came to my office because she was mad at a teacher she felt didn't like her. I told her I knew some things about this teacher that others in the building did not know. In my years at that middle school, this particular teacher would always come to me in private to find out what she could do to help students in need. Her family was well-to-do, but no one ever realized how graciously she gave to our students because she always did it anonymously. Though I did not tell Alicia the details, I explained I knew this teacher was one of the kindest in our building, and that if she would give her a chance, she would be surprised.

One thing I would say about Alicia was that she always listened to my advice and trusted me enough to consider the possibilities from our discussions. I was thrilled the day she came back and told me that I was right and that she had made friends with this teacher and found her to be supportive. Again a relationship was built, and that made all the difference.

As with most female students, eighth grade was filled with "girl issues." Our vice principal repeatedly had Alicia and two other girls in her office for fighting. Alliances within this small circle of friends were constantly changing, and often fist fights began in the cafeteria when their "war with words" got out of hand.

Alicia came to my office one day distraught over e-mails that were sent from her e-mail account to one of the other girls. She looked me straight in the eyes and said, "Ms. Doty, I didn't send this; I swear."

She thought another girl had gotten into her e-mail account and sent the messages to get her in trouble. By this time, we had a strong enough relationship that I knew she wouldn't lie.

Lo and behold, she was right. When discussing the situation with the other student, she admitted she had done this to get back at Alicia. I told our vice principal that I was going to take all three girls into my office, take out my hammer and nails, and finally get to the bottom of these disputes. I closed the door and hoped for the best. At that point, all I knew was that it was worth trying something different.

The three girls stared at me as we sat together around my half-moon table. There was clearly plenty of anger among them. Although it was difficult to decipher, I let them each express their versions of the disputes. Then I posed a question similar to the one I had asked Alicia when she was in seventh grade. I asked them what was difficult in their lives.

Although all unique, each story reflected dysfunction in their homes. How can young people know how to appropriately resolve conflict when there are no positive role models in their lives? This is also when you wish the public had more insight so better choices could be made regarding educational reforms. Perhaps then, we could really improve our students' quality of life which would be carried into adulthood.

After they had finished, I pointed out how much they needed each other. None of them had any support at home, so they needed their friendships more than most. With slightly softened expressions, they agreed that they wanted to be friends. I then revealed my old piece of 2x8 board, hammer, and nails, which definitely got their attention.

I created a different version of the story "The Fence," which is about a little boy with anger issues. His father suggested that whenever he felt angry, he should hammer nails into the fence. Finally, the little boy didn't need to hammer nails anymore; he had his anger under control. The dad then told his son to pull a nail every time he held his tongue and didn't lash out. Soon, all the nails were out of the fence. It was then the dad took the little boy to the fence, and they looked at all the nail holes. The dad explained that these were remnant scars left when things were said in anger.

I remember a teacher who shared with my night class the painful verbal abuse she endured over the years from her mother. She would be relieved when her mother slapped her across the face because the physical abuse signaled the end of each episode of verbal abuse. I realized the punches the girls threw in the cafeteria were far less damaging than the things they wrote and said to each other. I hoped the board and hammer would help them understand.

As I told a similar story with the girls as the main characters, Alicia pounded nails while the other two held the board. Then the nails were pulled out one by one. When we finished the story, we observed the board and talked about how they each had enough scars from people at home who had said and done things to them in anger. They did not need to add to it with the angry things they said to each other.

It was clear the girls were intrigued by the story, and it seemed to make the point. A few down the hall wondered what we were doing in the counseling office that day!

Later that year, things in Alicia's life continued a downward spiral. Her mother was back on drugs, her brother was in jail for drug abuse and other violations, and Alicia was now experimenting with drugs in an attempt to numb the pain. On two occasions, she confided to me that she no longer wanted to live.

Early one snowy morning, Alicia came to tell me about the woes of her life that particular week. Tears flowed as she described her ever-deepening depression. I told her we needed to assist her with attaining outside help. Though she didn't have a specific plan, she clearly did not want to continue living with all her pain.

I informed the vice principal of the call home I was going to make. The snow was accumulating quickly that morning, and by ten o'clock, we were told schools were being dismissed.

I called Alicia's mom from the vice principal's office. It was soon evident she was completely out of it when she answered the phone. Her response to my message that Alicia needed outside help was utterly unintelligible. I held the phone out so my vice principal could hear what I was listening to on the other end of the conversation. After ending the call and checking on Alicia, I noticed how bad the snow was getting outside. We discussed the need to call Social Services as it was clear Alicia's mom could be of no help.

Drew, now a seventh grade student and I nervously waited for nearly two hours for someone from Social Services to arrive and escort Alicia to our local mental health facility. Rather than sending a caseworker, Alicia's grandmother had been notified to come. She arrived despite the snowy conditions.

Drew and I quickly left school and barely made it across town to our home. We did not make it up our driveway on our first attempt. It was a fairly steep hill, and we ended up sideways in the grass on the first attempt, to the neighbor boy's amusement.

I ran up the hill and got a shovel, scooped away a little snow, threw some salt down and tried it again. We finally had success! Along with Katie, we settled in at home with pizza and a movie. Sadly, I wondered what Alicia was doing at that moment. She did not get to curl up under a quilt sharing the peaceful snow with her mom. Her mom could not even form a sentence.

Later I would discover that her mental health evaluation indicated that Alicia needed to be hospitalized for a few days. Then came the news that there were no rooms in any of the area facilities for Alicia. Her grandmother took her home that night and was instructed to watch her carefully until a bed opened somewhere.

I still feel anguish and rage when I recall this situation. Hundreds of thousands of dollars were being spent by the state to train teachers to drill objectives and for counselors to coordinate testing, yet we did not have a bed for a student who was in a life-threatening circumstance. It was unacceptable then, and still is today.

My work with Alicia and others students revealed how little the state of Virginia spent on mental health. They didn't need a task force when trying to find answers to the Virginia Tech shooting tragedy. Just talk to those in the trenches. We were expected to teach more standards every year with less time and money to do it, and yet so many students needed emotional support. Without emotional health as a priority, how could they be required to learn anything from a textbook?

Luckily, Alicia was eventually hospitalized before harming herself. These circumstances occurred more than once with other students in the four years I worked in that middle school. Family members should not be required to watch over a loved one until the appropriate help is available. We live in America, after all! We would not send someone home to wait for a bed if they were having a heart attack.

While spending a college semester abroad studying in Tanzania, Drew contracted malaria despite the medicine he took to avoid it. When his father and I lost contact with him over a weekend, we panicked. After numerous attempts to find answers and a sleepless night, Drew called to tell me he was very ill. He tried to reassure me that he was lucky because he was in Arusha and could pay to get the help he needed; however, that is not the case for so many in Africa.

Earlier during his trip, he encountered a sixteen-year-old Tanzanian girl who died of diabetes. Diabetics are lucky to live long in Tanzania with diets that consist mainly of starches, poor refrigeration for insulin, and the lack of money for proper medical care.

It did not occur to me until writing this chapter that what Drew described would not be surprising to most people when connected to Africa, yet they would never believe that medical help was not readily available to students in a mental health crisis in this country.

> "I lock my hands together before retreating inside my shell that will protect me for another day. Why? I sigh. If you are God, what is your reason? I just....I so badly want to know, Why? Why am I still alive?"
>
> -Dave Pelzer, *A Man Named Dave*

Later in the spring of Alicia's eighth grade year, she again suffered from severe depression. She sat in my rocking chair and described all of the atrocities occurring in her life. She cried so hard that day, she started to gag herself. I placed my waste basket beneath her as she double over in tears. I rubbed her back and told her to breathe deeply, hoping to calm her enough to understand what she was trying to say to me.

After several minutes, Alicia sat back, her face red and swollen, and said, "Ms. Doty am I God's experiment? Is He trying to see how much a person can take?"

What a humbling moment. I told her we weren't supposed to talk about our views about God in schools (which seemed ridiculous at such a moment), but that in my own life I, too, was going through great difficulties. I told her that it helped me to reframe my difficulties and think that perhaps God gave them to me so I could be a better counselor. In the midst of my very painful divorce when I began my middle school job three years earlier, I had often felt moments when life didn't seem worth living. I explained to Alicia I tried to use my hardships to better understand students' pain and suffering.

To that Alicia responded, "Well it is working, because you are a really good counselor."

I was amazed that in her time of immense distress she could be still be complimentary. Moments like that were what made Alicia so endearing to those who worked to help her.

Typically, a school counselor would not have the time to spend with Alicia that I devoted to her. Alicia's case was unusual because so often her needs were immediate and could not wait for her rare outside counseling appointments. It was clear the much-needed extensive therapy was never going to happen with this family. Jail time would become the ineffective remedy. I did my best to rearrange my schedule and stay late if needed so I could help Alicia on her many bad days.

On that particular afternoon, Alicia eventually calmed down enough so we could talk. Her answer to a question I posed nearly a decade ago still brings tears to my eyes. I asked her to describe what would be her perfect day.

She contemplated the question for a moment and said, "I would be coming downstairs from my bedroom in the morning, and my mom would be cooking me breakfast. Our house would have a picket fence in the front of it."

That was it; that was all it took to make a perfect day for her. She didn't long to win a lottery or go on an exotic vacation; she simply wanted to get up to her mom making breakfast. It was one of the simplest of things which most of us take for granted during childhood. I often reminded Katie and Drew that even on our worst days, we were still lucky and had a great deal for which to be grateful. I will always be thankful to Alicia for teaching me so much about human frailty, resilience, and perseverance.

- 23 -
The Testing Interruption

Throughout the four years I worked in the middle school in Virginia, the state progressed from testing one subject in seventh grade and two in eighth grade, to testing numerous subjects in all sixth through eighth grades. I coordinated over twenty two hundred online tests the last year I was there.

To set up online testing, we used the media center, chorus room, and all computer labs. This required a great deal of school personnel's time. Scheduling, running test receipts, sorting, and stuffing envelopes were just a few of the necessary tasks.

During testing weeks, I wore comfortable clothes and a pair of sneakers because with the new online testing paired with our old equipment, we inevitably had test sessions shut down when students were in the middle of an exam. I would get one panicked walkie-talkie message after another stating a test had gone down. Naturally, this would cause stress for students and teachers alike. During the month of testing insanity, I was so busy I did not have time to address personal issues with students.

Taxpayers do not realize the amount of money and manpower they fund for state-mandated testing. As a taxpayer myself, I want to see teachers teach and counselors counsel. But again, every year with school personnel cuts, what we really slash are the valuable services we are hired to perform.

One year testing time arrived when we had a rush of students who were "cutting" and another student who had lost a parent. I was so frustrated I couldn't give the appropriate time and attention to these students in need. I would not have imagined that so many girls develop "cutting" issues at such a young age until I worked with middle school students. It seemed that once the idea of "cutting" to relieve emotional tension surfaced, many tried it to relieve their own pain. I felt helpless because I knew responding to these issues as they arose was not effective; we needed to also focus our efforts on prevention.

Again, here was evidence for the need for comprehensive school counseling curriculum that addressed appropriate ways to relieve stress. School counselors fight for every minute of time they are allowed in classrooms, and understandably so. Teachers' jobs are now on the line based on test results and they have many interruptions to their teaching time already. What a difference we could make if we just rearranged the priorities in education.

One year I had a seventh grade girl carve "I hate my mom" on her upper thigh. It was a deep, lasting set of scars. I wasn't able to reach her before she injured herself in this way. Her leg will always bear the message, especially when she goes swimming and her skin tans, leaving the scarred communication for all to see. It goes without saying her mom was unfit, and she was simply trying to announce her pain to the world.

Once again, I found myself trying to convince Social Services to get to my student's home immediately because her mom had a knife and was out of control. Later, I was checking out at a personal doctor's appointment when a caseworker returned the call I had made before leaving school that day. All eyes in the waiting room were on me as I gathered my belongings and headed to the parking lot to finish my tense conversation.

I wanted to return to the waiting room when I completed the call and challenge those inside to please call their lawmakers and demand change in public education. Throw out state testing, let teachers create their own assessments, and use those financial resources for situation like this one. Most would never believe the amount of drug use, sex, drinking, gay bashing, "cutting," and abuse from home that we confront on a regular basis in schools. Young people are having babies with no coping skills. I am still astounded how often and early it begins.

The Testing Interruption

- 24 -
Leaving Virginia

Seven years of school counseling in Virginia left me burned out. I loved the counseling work and students, but when you are grappling with a system that is headed in the wrong direction, it was defeating. Not wanting to make any drastic changes in my personal life immediately after my divorce, I stayed in Virginia for several years before making the decision to move to Colorado to be closer to family and have a fresh start. Katie was in college at the time and Drew just finishing his freshman year of high school.

I let Drew decide whether he wanted to stay with his father in Virginia to finish high school or move with me. I acted brave but knew deep-down I would never be able to leave him. He decided to move with me, and so we set off on pure faith as I had no job in Colorado and a house to sell in Virginia! We packed up and said our difficult goodbyes to friends and family. The challenges that lay ahead were uncharted, but we hoped for better days in Colorado.

I will never forget my many dear friends and colleagues in Virginia who continue to work diligently on behalf of the children, despite the uncompromising constraints of a system that is obsessed with testing. I have great admiration for those who still try their best for students in the midst of all that is wrong.

I return each year to Virginia to visit friends. They update me on the students we worried about and tried to help. Most are not positive outcomes as these children were left behind both at home and at school.

But in Virginia and most states, test scores are
still the only thing that matter.

– 25 –
Colorado

I quickly worked to clean the last bathroom after showering the night before Drew and I were to leave for our long journey. Emotions were overwhelming, to say the least. The next thing I knew, I jammed my pinky finger into the side of the sink while wiping it down. I felt the jarring pain and knew it was bad. It is still hard for me to believe that I was so wound-up I could break a finger on the side of a sink. But then again, the point of all I write is the power of our emotions and the effects they have on all we do in life.

My finger throbbed, and when I lowered it to my side, I could not stand the pain. I sobbed from both heartache and physical pain. Katie followed me stuffing everything left in the house into my car. I needed to have all my financial records, computers and other items which could not go on the moving van with me, so by this time, the car was completely full. Katie managed to shove all the remaining items into the back seat as we both wept. I had imagined all the goodbyes, but I never envisioned what it would be like to close the door to our home. It was a symbolic end to our family and a moment full of great sadness.

I drove our packed car next door where I would stay with friends the final evening. Drew was with his dad the previous night. It was very clear how painful their goodbye had been when he came through the neighbor's door that dark, rainy evening. It was the one moment I questioned my decision to leave, my faith being greatly tested.

I write about these painful memories because I have so many personal reasons for wishing we prioritized the teaching of emotional intelligence in schools. I will always wonder how things might have been different for my own family.

That night I lay awake in my neighbor's home in perhaps the greatest physical and emotional pain of my life. I could not get any relief from pain medication for my finger, and nothing was going to help the fear and sadness in my heart. I felt panicked because I knew I had to do all the driving and I wasn't getting any sleep. How could I stay awake? The trip to Nebraska and Colorado each summer for visits had gotten more difficult every year as I found I would often get so tired. Now here I was in so much pain and absolutely wiped out from the emotional exhaustion of the prior weeks. Emotional exhaustion is truly the most tiring of all.

Morning came and was filled with memories as I tried to eat some breakfast before we said that final goodbye to our neighbors. They had become like surrogate grandparents when we moved to Virginia ten years earlier. I remembered our first day in Virginia. Jerry was happily out mowing his yard at his usual speedy pace, and stopped to greet us. We felt excited to have such a friendly neighbor. We left the next morning to take Katie and Drew for their first day of school.

That day in Virginia was Drew's first day of kindergarten. He bravely entered his classroom without any tears. We went to the cafeteria to pay for the kids' lunch accounts, and the cafeteria supervisor kindly explained the system and then informed us about "grandparents day" which was held in October. The wall came tumbling down, and I started crying as I explained that all of our grandparents were in Nebraska and wouldn't be able to come.

I had left Nebraska saying all my goodbyes without a tear. It was simply too overwhelming to allow the feelings to surface. My grandmother's entire body shook as I hugged her goodbye. She had bone marrow cancer, and I could not bear the thought that this would be our last goodbye. She knew it would be.

Mike looked at me in surprise at this outburst of emotion. We walked down the hall to exit, and there came Drew's class. I knew I couldn't let him see me crying, or he might become upset as well. I put on a red-faced, puffy-eyed smile as we passed him, and luckily he didn't notice I had been weeping.

When we arrived home, the movers were waiting for us and trying to figure out how to maneuver our steep driveway with their trucks. We got to the top of the driveway, and we were met by Jerry's wife, Donna. She had a plate of cookies and their phone number on a sticky note in case we needed it for anything. Then she asked us what time we wanted our dinner. That was all it took for the flood gates to open again, and I cried at the kindness of our new neighbors.

Now, Jerry was ill with cancer as we said our final, tearful goodbyes. We made it a few miles out of town and I pulled the car off the road to try to gain my composure. Nothing I ever learned in school prepared me for this difficult time in my life. I wished I knew how to handle the pain of our broken family.

Drew and I continued down the beautiful, winding Virginia road. After an hour, I had to stop and try to find a splint for my finger which was throbbing and swollen. Drew convinced me he could drive as he was fifteen and needed to learn, anyway. So, he took the wheel as we traveled through the countryside, and I drove through the major cities. I tried to keep my finger elevated and wrapped with ice to control the pain.

Looking back, I should have stopped for some medical treatment. However, the movers were supposedly on our heels headed for Colorado, and I had a few things I wanted to do in our new home before all the furniture arrived, so we kept a steady pace. The decisions we make when in severe emotional grief and stress are never well thought-out. Drew and I were lucky we made the long journey safely. Ironically, the movers did not arrive with all of our belongings until almost two weeks later! We needed our belongings, and the two week wait seemed like an eternity.

I remembered these feelings while watching news reports about the people in Colorado who lost their homes the past summer of 2012 to the raging fires in the record-setting summer heat. It is incredibly difficult to lose your home and all of your material possessions. While human life is always most important, the material things with which we choose to surround ourselves bring comfort. Losing all that is cherished brings immense grief.

I stood with my parents and sister's family on our new Colorado driveway the day our moving truck finally arrived and watched as the movers lifted the door on the back of the truck. Though poorly packed and much damaged in the fiasco of the weeks prior, the sight of some of our familiar things brought reassurance and tears.

Soon boxes were piled throughout our new house leaving little room to even walk around. Despite the pain of my finger which I discovered weeks later was broken, I unpacked things at a record pace because it felt so good to be surrounded again with the things that meant "home" to us. My new neighbor was surprised at the number of flattened boxes I stacked in our driveway. It was hard to believe that despite the purging I had done in Virginia, I still had so much to unpack. Life in Colorado had begun.

I registered Drew for high school, and as I drove away from his school that first day, I prayed he would make new friends quickly. I couldn't imagine how scary it must have been for him. I came back to a quiet house. I had left a job that was both satisfying and overwhelming and was now faced with silence and uncertainty.

Now I had nothing to do but worry. *When would my home in Virginia sell? When would I get a job? How would I pay the bills? Was Katie okay in college out East? Would Drew be happy in Colorado?*

The next year of life was an unfamiliar existence. There were so many moments of utter fear and loneliness. I had started to write this book while in Virginia and kept thinking I should take the extra time to finish it. I love to read and also reminded myself that I had the time to do it, but the fear and panic kept me from feeling like I should allow myself those luxuries.

I wanted to do some substitute teaching, but learned that the local school system would not allow it until Colorado had issued my teaching and counseling licenses. Having license reciprocity with Virginia did nothing to expedite this process. It took the state three long, agonizing months to send my license. No one at the Department of Education cared that they were holding up the livelihood of a single mother.

– 26 –
Highly Qualified

I spent four years working full-time in middle school in Virginia before moving to Colorado. I had no formal training for middle school counseling, but I also had a K-8 teaching certificate. During those four years when the No Child Left Behind legislation was passed, I was suddenly stripped of my ability to teach 6-8 because I was not considered "highly qualified" in middle school subjects.

It seemed so unfair that with the flick of a pen, a portion of the teaching degree I had earned was now useless. Yet no one cared about my counseling degree which just had middle school counseling added to it. Virginia did not have a K-6 counseling license; therefore my new license was for K-8 school counseling. I was also able to add high school counseling when renewing my license the year before I left Virginia for twenty five dollars: ironic. "Highly qualified" is one of the most ridiculous aspects of the No Child Left Behind legislation in that it ensures nothing in terms quality of instruction.

While I am proud of the degrees I have earned, the letters behind my name have nothing to do with my effectiveness as a teacher or counselor. In that first year of teaching after graduating from college, I was a Chapter One tutor. I worked with a first grade teacher who had a master's degree in teaching reading. On paper she was "highly qualified" as defined by federal standards. In reality, she should never have been allowed in a classroom.

When I visited each teacher that year to find out if they had any students who could benefit from extra tutoring, she explained she had ten students she wanted me to work with on reading skills. She then pointed to her front row where ten students sat looking up at us as she proclaimed, "This is what I call my dumb shit row."

I could not believe my ears. I wanted to shed all of my emotional intelligence at that moment and deck her. Sadly, the principal did nothing when I reported this occurrence.

A few years later, I worked with an outstanding teacher. Mary could garner students' attention; she could teach large groups, small groups, and everything in-between. She had an amazing way of presenting material and involving students. The teacher next door couldn't hold the attention of our students for any length of time. When the students entered her room for math instruction, their behaviors immediately deteriorated and would instantly improve when they returned to our room.

I felt it would have been more effective to keep our room self-contained with such young students, but I was the new one on the block with little voice. Luckily, I had Mary helping me. Ironically, she was not a "highly qualified" teacher. She was our classroom aide. Make no mistake: "highly qualified" does not guarantee quality.

While I do not doubt that having some formal training in counseling at the secondary level would have helped me those first few months, the ultimate measure of success would be directly related to my determination, passion, and motivation. These traits in addition to genuine concern and a strong work ethic are what make an effective counselor.

These same traits dictated my effectiveness as a teacher. I believe I could have been a very successful middle school teacher while in Virginia despite not being "highly qualified" as defined by the new legislation. A good teacher can interpret learning standards, and then use best practices to teach them. Highly qualified teachers, in my view, are the ones who know how to develop relationships in their rooms; the rest will follow!

A story that must be told in context of "highly qualified" educators is that of Mrs. Brown. My mom worked part-time before she retired as the volunteer coordinator for her local school district. Teachers submitted what their particular needs were, and my mom would match them with a volunteer. She was a natural recruiter and grew a program that serviced her district with thousands of volunteer hours in addition to a living history program that won the Ike Friedman Community Leadership Award from the Knights of Arksarben.

Mom had a request from a special education teacher for someone to work one-on-one with a ninth grade boy who wanted to quit school but was not old enough. Sam was unsuccessful in school because he could not read and write as a result of his dyslexia. He had received all the special services provided by the district in previous years, but still was not reading and writing proficiently enough to stay caught up with his peers and his classes.

Mom matched him with Mrs. Brown who had no experience in teaching but had raised many children over the years, both her own as well as a multitude of foster children. With Mrs. Brown's children grown and her best friend recently passing away, she needed something in her life to fill the voids. She had seen an article Mom had written in the local newspaper telling about the volunteer program and the need for more volunteers.

She called mom, and that began a relationship that would transform two lives. Mrs. Brown was an older woman that by appearances, would probably not relate well with this young man. However, Mom felt that if so many foster children had been placed in her home over the years, it was worth a try.

Late on the first day with Sam, Mrs. Brown called Mom to tell her how she had put her finger under each word as he slowly read along. She said that she had discovered he was a very capable learner and able to discuss what he had read with her.

Often learning disabled children are not viewed as intelligent because their disabilities hinder their ability to keep up. Additionally, a great deal of energy is used to compensate for the disability. Yet once they've mastered coping strategies, they can fulfill their true learning potential.

Later in the year, Sam baked Mrs. Brown cookies for Valentine's Day and brought them to school to give to her. A relationship and bond had been built. At the end of the year, he said he would come back the next year if she would also come back. This became an annual ritual until he was a senior.

On the last day Mrs. Brown was to work with Sam, she was called to the office. She was worried she had done something wrong. Perhaps she had parked her car in the wrong place? Sam's family, so thrilled he was about to graduate, had sent Mrs. Brown a beautiful bouquet of flowers with a note of gratitude. They credited her for being the sole reason Sam would graduate.

Sam had given Mrs. Brown purpose in her life again and in return, she taught Sam to read and write. With no teaching experience, much less "highly qualified" credentials, Mrs. Brown changed a life forever. The importance of having time to build one-on-one relationships with struggling students is paramount, yet with the ever-increasing curriculum standards and larger class sizes resulting from budget cuts, this is impossible in most classrooms.

After spending many long days which turned into months searching and applying for jobs, my teaching license finally arrived from the Colorado Department of Education. I began substitute teaching with the hope of finding a full-time job for the following school year. In May a high school counseling job offer came, and some relief for my financial situation! It would not be until the following March that my home in Virginia would finally sell.

Highly Qualified

- 27 -
High School

I began my new job both excited and nervous; never having worked with high school students, I didn't know what to expect. Soon, I realized just how much I didn't know about my new job. I dragged home stacks of information each day. I spent my evenings learning all I could about scheduling, graduation requirements, college admissions, financial aid, names of staff, students, district personnel, and community resources.

I quickly found out how much I enjoyed working with high school students. Just as in elementary and middle school, I encountered motivated students, unmotivated students, and everything in-between. They, too, had their individual stories of success and triumph, sadness, loss, and resilience.

High schools have a different "feel" though, than other levels in education. This is largely because students have different teachers each period of the day for the many subject areas. It is difficult to form bonding relationships in this structure and can leave students feeling less connected to the institution as a whole. It takes strong leadership and organization to create a welcoming atmosphere at all levels, but especially at the high school level.

I remember Katie commenting during her high school years that no one cared. I'm sure this sentiment is felt by many high school students. The larger the school, the greater the challenge in creating a caring atmosphere, and it cannot be accomplished without the adults in the building leading the way. This, too, is part of **the forgotten education**. Interpersonal skills will always make or break a leader and his or her organization.

With Katie's sentiments regarding feeling "uncared for" while in high school in mind, I worked hard to overcome my insecurities so I could be sensitive to the needs of my students. This is a challenge we all face in education. The more budgets are cut, the more stressful jobs in education become. It is natural for people to become somewhat "narcissistic" when they have so much on their plates, or when they are in times of crisis. The world becomes "all about us" when we are overwhelmed with stress. When were we ever taught "stress management?" What could be more important in our fast-paced, information-overloaded world?

"I was gratified to be able to answer promptly, and I did. I said I didn't know."

-Mark Twain

That first year, I had more questions than answers for the students who came to the Career Center where I worked part of the week. I wasn't afraid to say, "I don't know, but I'll find out." My poor co-workers must have been exhausted as I relied heavily upon them for many of the answers.

One senior girl came to see me often in the Career Center as she was on her own throughout high school. Her mom was a severe alcoholic and seldom attended events for her daughter and when she did, she often embarrassed her daughter. We worked through the college admissions process together that fall, both of us learning as we went. I had to remind myself often that the most important thing was to convey I cared, not how much or, in my case, how little I knew.

December came quickly and before the holiday break, our Student Council members wrote their annual letters to staff. Each member of the faculty receives a hand-written note from a member of the Student Council thanking them for their service to our school.

I will never forget how surprised I was when reading my letter. It is still on my bulletin board at home as a reminder of what is important in these stressful times of education. It came from the girl I had assisted in the Career Center that fall. Her words were such a gift to me in all my uncertainty: "It is amazing to us seniors that this is your first year here. You are so respected, and many of us do not have anyone to care for us."

Showing others how much we care must always be the first priority. It trumps everything else, although it can be difficult when we are overwhelmed.

One of the highlights of our high school was the Little Café run by one of our special education teachers. She integrated core subject areas with real-life learning as the students were taught to plan, budget, shop, cook, and use good interpersonal skills serving in the café. Teachers would race each week for a coveted Thursday lunch reservation.

When I first experienced the café, I knew immediately this was an example of master teaching. It was creative, challenging, and most of all, relevant to real life and the standards that were being taught. If you had a reservation for their once-a-week café experience, you would receive a phone call the day before from one of the students confirming it. Upon entering the café, you were met with a soothing ambiance that was created by tables donned with pretty white table cloths, soft music, and Christmas tree lights lining the decorative, painted walls. A student greeted you at the door and took you to your table.

Soon after being seated, another student server took your drink order. Pitchers of both ice water and tea were served by students who wore a white linen cloth over their serving arms. Salad with rolls and butter were brought as the first course, followed by the main dish. The final course included a delicious dessert accompanied with a cup of hot coffee or tea. Best of all, we enjoyed the special treat of spending rare "down time" with colleagues.

The students were each assigned duties in the cafeteria and at the conclusion of our meal, they lined up and introduced themselves. We were given an evaluation card to fill out to help improve their service. Again, it was one of the most amazing learning environments in our school. It was integrated, creative, and most of all, relevant to real-life skill development. New graduation requirements threatened this valuable program. The lead teacher would have attempted to rescue the program had she stayed on staff. It ended with her retirement.

I volunteered to be a part of our district crisis team. We never know when we will be called to respond. Of course, the "what" you will be responding to is always the most challenging part. While difficult to serve on such a team, I would rather be involved than sitting at home watching crisis unfold on the television. Writing of this educational memoir has also been difficult, but hopefully gives voice to the inescapable truth that we need more than test scores to measure how well we educate our youth. Emotional illiteracy often costs us lives.

When responding to the suicide death of a young middle school girl a few years ago, I was asked to read a written announcement regarding the death in the classrooms. Though serving on district crisis teams many prior years, this was something I had never done before. The message written by the principal was short and simply announced the death and the name of the young female student. It was not appropriate to release the cause of the death at that time. Those who work with middle school students understand the constant motion and interaction inherent with the age. This day all was still.

Class by class, I introduced myself and told them I was a school counselor, and their principal had asked me to help him that afternoon. I explained that unfortunately, we had sad news to tell them. I read the two-line announcement that the principal had scripted. I offered respite areas that were staffed with other volunteers to the students if they felt they wanted to leave the classroom. We explained that the remainder of the class time was theirs to talk with friends or teachers while processing the sad announcement.

As I moved from room to room, a few students raised their hands to ask what had happened. In the modern age of technology, students usually find out details before the adults but all phones were off that day. It was the silence that I remember most about that day. Two of us made our way through the sixth and seventh grade rooms. We stayed for a short time after each announcement and then moved on to the next room.

After I had completed this, I went back to the first room where I had left my intern. Students were still sitting in silence. No one seemed to know what to do next. My intern was as uncomfortable as I. We had anticipated students would want to talk as they processed the news. Instead, we faced the uncharacteristic silence.

Those most affected had been taken to another location with a volunteer who told them of the news. In those locations, there were many tears and much discussion, but in the classrooms, only silence and sadness on the faces of fellow middle school students.

The state standards that were to be taught that day had little significance. One of their classmates had died.

The absurdity of pacing guides with mandates directing the exact timing for teaching objectives always comes to my mind when in crisis situations. When do we allow students and staff the basic human need for grief?

In retrospect, bringing in the trained therapy dogs to walk through the aisles of silent students would have been very beneficial. I had responded to this school another year when there was a student death and sat with students in the library with the therapy dog and his owner. It was amazing to observe the positive effect an animal can have in these situations. These dogs sense their purpose and unconditionally offer their quiet affection to those in need. The owners are careful to allow their dogs to respond for only specified time limits. Even with animals, the emotional toll is great in these situations. Sadly, we don't tend to the human responders as responsibly. With so many aspects of education, we do the best we can with the resources available. And in the case of crisis management, there is no money allotted. Crisis team members all volunteer. They return to their school settings after each crisis and attempt to catch up on their stressful workloads.

I had to find my own ways to de-brief after that long afternoon. As my own crisis mode melted into exhaustion that evening, and I processed the sadness, I again felt the familiar surge of anger at the lawmakers who simply do NOT get it. They don't realize what happens when they pass legislation requiring more and more of teachers and students. We simply do not have the time to be human.

They do not have to look into the eyes of young students who have just heard the news of a classmate's death. They don't close their eyes at night with fresh trauma in their minds and the thoughts of the families that will never be the same again. Crisis is an unavoidable part of life. Responding to crisis is always a difficult thing. But responding to crisis that might have been avoided with more time and attention given to the emotional issues of our young people should not have to be tolerated.

> "Defeat is not the worst of failures. Not to have tried is the true failure."
>
> —Jill Doty

This book may lie on only a few shelves collecting dust and has certainly taken me a very long time to finish, but to "not try" to communicate the message is failure. We owe to ourselves and our children to advocate for **the forgotten education**.

- 28 -
Drugs and Alcohol
"The Helpers"

I struggle as I attempt to convey my final thoughts. There are so many stories left untold and those that unfold each day that passes. We lost our way in education long before the **No Child Left Behind** Act was passed. Unfortunately, instead of turning the bus around, this legislation has sent it full-speed ahead to the edge of a cliff. There have been so many victims along the way, and there will be masses of victims when the dust has settled from the crash. I must share some final stories before concluding this written journey.

It was a bright, sunny Wednesday morning in Colorado. Wednesdays are shortened days for students to allow time for staff collaboration. I was busy working in my office when I heard shuffling noises outside my doorway. I looked up to see a student on a gurney; paramedics were taking the student out to the ambulance through the side door. With the nurse's office a part of our counseling department, I have a front row seat to scenes such as this far too often.

After the paramedics left, I wondered if once again, it was a student who had overdosed on drugs or alcohol. It was a scene that I had witnessed before, but one that is never discussed. Now, working in a high school, I find this story has far too many chapters.

Once while working in the middle school in Virginia, I assisted a seventh grade boy who was hyperventilating in the nurse's office. The nurse was trying to reach his mom to come take him home. She informed me that she thought he had strep throat. I went to see him and could not believe the state he was in. He lay breathing rapidly and blinking uncontrollably. The nurse had commented on his bad breath. When I spoke with him, I could smell the unusual odor.

I immediately remembered a presentation I had heard not long before about meth use and its signs and symptoms. I asked the nurse to step into the hall and suggested the possibility that these were symptoms of meth use. She had only worked in elementary schools before coming to our middle school and could not fathom a seventh grade boy on meth, but she had to admit he did exhibit symptoms. I had heard this young boy's mother was a drug addict, adding to my suspicions about his symptoms. The day ended with another unproductive call to Social Services.

A few hours after the paramedics took one of our high school students out on a gurney, I heard more commotion outside my office. Unbelievably, I saw another student on a gurney being carried out by the paramedics. Later I asked the nurse if overdosing had anything to do with the two students who left on the gurneys that day.

She said, "Yes," and then described the various methods students were using to deal with stress. We discussed our common concerns about the issues students face along with the ignorance of the public regarding these situations.

That afternoon we were reviewing "data" as a staff. Two students had left on gurneys that morning, yet the routine conversations addressing academic interventions still transpired. Ironically, there were no discussions concerning emotional interventions.

Improving test scores doesn't matter to students on gurneys.

The presence of "helpers" (alcohol and drugs) in our schools is nothing new. Having worked with students of all ages, I have found them to be very grateful when they can access the services of their school counselor. My ongoing frustrations worsen each year as more irrelevant tasks are added to my position. Knowing the "helpers" are readily available while I spend time on these mundane tasks instead of counseling is exasperating.

"Helpers" are present at every level of education, but clearly, high schools are inundated with drug and alcohol abuse. Students' schedules allow them the freedom to engage in the use of "helpers" more readily than in elementary or middle school students.

Instead of forming connections with people, students bond with their "helpers" of choice, and quite often these relationships last well beyond high school. Universities and colleges have been noted for the prevalence of "helpers" for decades, but sadly, drug and alcohol use has now permeated secondary education.

Should we really be leaving "the helpers" with the responsibility of filling the huge voids of **the forgotten education**? Our youth are not given the tools needed to resist the appeal of the "helpers." Too often, addiction is the unfortunate result. Our infants receive well-baby check-ups and are vaccinated against many serious illnesses. Yet, very little is done to ward off the disease of addiction.

Joseph A. Caifrano, Jr., Chairman and President of the National Center on Addiction and Substanse Abuse at Columbia University and former U.S. Secretary of Health, Education, and Welfare states, "A major shift in American attitudes about substance abuse and addiction and a top to bottom overhaul in the nation's health care, criminal justice, social service, and education systems, and awakening the power of parenting, to curtail the rise in illegal drug use and other substance abuse."

The National Center on Addiction and Substance Abuse reports on their website that almost "a quarter of a trillion of the nation's yearly health care bill is attributable to substance abuse and addiction."

"Helpers" are in high demand as our students face stresses that are unique from previous generations. The dawn of the internet and social media, the rate and change of knowledge, the rising divorce rates and broken families, and the pressure to perform in school, all contribute to these tremendous stressors. Students have access to the world with a touch of their phones.

While amazing, this super-highway of information can also be overwhelming and destructive. We do not teach youth how to handle this exposure. We do not guide them about when it is time to shut the world off and be present with people. And we are still subjecting them to tests modeled on an educational system developed during the Industrial Age.

Although the rate and change of knowledge is increasing at an unbelievable pace, little has changed in education. Students do not need to memorize what they can access with a brush of their fingertips. What they do need is the ability to process events. They need time and opportunities to think critically and discuss deeply. And they need the skills to apply what they learn in real-life situations.

Accompanying these challenges are frustrated teachers who endure hours of training to understand a twenty-seven page evaluation tool that will be used to assess their skills. Fifty percent of the evaluation will be student growth. Yet no one has figured out exactly how to measure that growth. No one has figured out how this will be a fair comparison when some teachers teach top level courses where students generally come motivated to do well, and others teach the classes filled with many students who never even come to class. No one has figured out what to do when teachers demand the removal of unprepared students from their classes—the "unwanted" who reflect poorly on evaluations of all kinds.

This is public education, and a student has the right to take any class they want regardless of the appropriate prerequisites. So what is a teacher to do with a student who failed a math class and is now in a class that builds upon the knowledge of that previous class? What should be done when students are passed on to the next level in English without successfully mastering the previous level? It is easy to say we need to stop social promotion, but if this is truly instituted, we could end up with first graders who are ready to begin shaving.

There is never just one factor to explain a student's lack of academic success. Illness, hunger, lack of parenting, learning disabilities, overloaded classes, lack of differentiation, and ineffective teachers, can all be contributing factors, and the list goes on. If we could finally come to this realization, we could then provide the appropriate interventions. We do not adequately prepare teachers to understand the whole child. All school personnel training programs should include comprehensive training regarding the connection between the affective, psychomotor, and cognitive domains in learning. This is the first step in understanding what interventions are needed for each individual student.

In addition, we need the support of school counselors who are allowed time for individual and group counseling. It is time to stop diluting the role of school counselors with non-counseling duties. It is time we value the counselor role as an authentic academic intervention.

Solutions for academic failure have resulted in the development of more rigorous standards. However, rigor and standardized education are simply an oxymoron. Standardization is learning the same thing at the same rate; rigor increases challenge. In the pursuit to standardize learning, the goal is to ensure that everyone can reach the same level of mastery at the same time which compromises rigor, remediation, differentiation, relevance, and creativity. Sadly, administrators who demand standardization as well as rigor simply don't recognize the amazing contradiction. Asking our students to be alike (standardized) and unique (creative) are on absolute opposite ends of the educational spectrum.

Teachers need help in their classrooms. With every student added to a class roster, the teacher becomes less effective. In all situations, the more you have to do, quality and value are compromised.

My best friend from high school just returned to full-time teaching after twenty one years, and she describes the incredible amounts of curriculum she is expected to teach. She has twenty seven students in her third grade classroom, many with very unique and time consuming needs. She spends hours and hours outside her work day trying to keep up with all the planning and paperwork. What I experienced as a young teacher in the early eighties is now an even worse situation. **The forgotten education** is more apparent than ever with the increasing curriculum demands and budget cuts.

And now sadly, before I could complete the final draft of this book, another horrific school shooting has occurred. Sandy Hook Elementary School was the scene of yet another school shooting massacre in December of 2012.

Again, I wring my hands and want to shout from the mountain tops! We do not prioritize mental health in our society! We do not address emotional intelligence in schools! We are too consumed with standards! The media reports that perhaps mental health IS the story with the Sandy Hook shooting. Of course, the gun control debate dominates the conversation along with the ridiculous notion we should "arm" our teachers. I think of all the lives lost from "friendly fire" by trained military personnel when in combat. In the midst of crisis, things get confused and sometimes the "good guy" gets killed even with our well-trained military troops. I can't imagine how many innocent people could be killed if we "armed" an entire school staff.

After Sandy Hook, fear replaced common sense, and my dear high school friend was expected to take turns with her colleagues "guarding" the school's front door during their plan times. Ovewhelmed teachers, without enough help or time to teach increible amounts of curriculum, were expected to sacrifice plan time sitting at the front door of their school. Any of them would be willing to do anything to make their students safer, as were the teachers at Sandy Hook Elementary School. But sitting at the door without even so much a walkie-talkie for communication does nothing to make students and staff safer.

The district has since hired personnel to sit in the entry area of every school where the main office is not at the front door. This procedure would have done nothing to stop the Sandy Hook shooting, yet money is spent out of emotion, not reason. We all want to feel safe but know that ultimately, if someone really wants to go on a killing spree, short of holding up in forts surrounded by motes and armed guards, they will be successful.

I would like to "arm" my students with emotional intelligence skills to prepare them for the real world. One of our local school resource officers stated in a newspaper article shortly after the Sandy Hook shooting, that students are much more at risk because of their personal "high risk" choices. "The helpers" take even more lives in much quieter, less obvious ways.

Mary Cathryn Ricker, President of the St. Paul Federation of Teachers said it best in her blog entry following:

A Blog Entry By Mary Cathryn Ricker

You want to arm me? Good. Then arm me with a school psychologist at my school who has time...to do more than test and sit in meetings about testing.

Arm me with enough counselors so we can build skills to prevent violence, have meaningful discussions with students about their future and not merely frantically adjust student schedules like a Jenga game.

Arm me with social workers who can thoughtfully attend to a student's and her family's needs so I. Can. Teach.

Arm me with enough school nurses so that they are accessible to every child and can work as a team with me rather than operate their offices as de facto urgent care centers.

Arm me with more days on the calendar for teaching and learning and fewer days for standardized testing.

Arm me with class sizes that allow my colleagues and I to know both our students and their families well.

Arm my colleagues and me with the time it takes to improve together and the time it takes to give great feedback to students about their work and progress.

Until you arm me to the hilt with what it will take to meet the needs of an increasingly vulnerable student population, I respectfully request you keep your opinions on schools and our safety to yourself NRA. Knock it off.

185

I recently endured a sleepless night distressed by the thoughts from a conversation I had that evening with a friend. She described the senseless death of a young man who had lost his battle with alcohol addiction. He did not possess skills in coping with his emotions. "The helpers" took over his life. He is gone forever with only the pledge made the day before his death, to try to free himself from "the helpers," left for those who loved him.

It is time to put a halt to this endless trail of children left behind who grow to become dysfunctional adults. We must recognize the connection to a curriculum greatly lacking in emotional literacy.

Consider again the words of Daniel Goleman author of *Emotional Intelligence*: "If character development is a foundation of democratic societies, consider some of the ways emotional intelligence buttresses this foundation. The bedrock of character is self-discipline: the virtuous life, as philosophers since Aristotle have observed, is based on self-control."

And Herbert Spencer, the great philosopher, stating over a hundred years ago, "Education has for its object the formation of character."

Theodore Roosevelt said, "To educate a man in mind and not in morals is to educate a menace to society."

And, Abraham Lincoln declared, "The philosophy of the school room in one generation will be the philosophy of government in the next."

With both political parties in consideration, Lincoln's words resonate. We do not teach how to play nice in the sand box anymore, and it is very evident in our government.

Kenneth Kenniston was quoted in David Elkind's book *The Hurried Child* as saying, "We measure the success of schools not by the kinds of human beings they promote but by whatever increases in reading scores they chalk up. We have allowed quantitative standards, so central to the adult economic system, to become the principal yardstick for our definition of our children's worth."

If the goal of education is to teach students the skills necessary to be productive and contributing citizens of our society, when do they learn the social skills **most** necessary for this outcome? When do we teach them how to communicate, to have self control, to handle rejection, to grieve, and to problem solve? When do we teach them how to manage stress, peer pressure, bullying, cyberspace, relationships, and most of all, their feelings? When do we start comprehensive prevention programs necessary to protect them from "the helpers?"

These **forgotten lessons** need to be more than brief encounters in educational institutions. They need to be integrated into every part of the educational environment, and emotional intelligence needs a front seat position next to all core subjects. Now more than ever, I believe that if we start by teaching students how to get along with others, the rest will follow.

Who are "the children left behind?" They are the ones education labeled as failures based on their tests scores rather than providing inspiration and guidance in discovering their strengths. They are those who suffer from abuse. They are those who abuse. They are those sitting in our prisons. They are those in families embroiled in generations of dysfunction. They are those who are addicted to drugs, alcohol, consumerism, and eating. They are parents who put their own needs ahead of their children's. They are those who have no idea how to manage their emotions.

They are those in the news every day. They are those whose silent pain will never make the news. They are represented in every race, color, gender, and socioeconomic group.

It is my greatest hope that some of the stories in this book will inspire you to take action and communicate with lawmakers regarding **the forgotten education**. I hope you begin recognizing the voids in education which have allowed "the helpers" to consume our society. It is time to understand what it means to all of us *when children are left behind*.

The Children Left Behind

Recommended Reading

Elkind, David (1988). *The Hurried Child*. New York: Addison-Wesley Publishing Company, Inc.

Glenn, Stephen H., Nelsen, Jane Ed. D. (1989). *Raising Self-Reliant Children In A Self-Indulgent World*. Rocklin, CA: Prima Publishing & Communications

Goleman, Daniel (1995). *Emotional Intelligence*. New York: Bantam Books

Hannaford, Carla Ph.D. (2005). *Smart Moves*. Salt Lake City UT: Great River Books

Healy, Jane M., Ph.D. (1990). *Endangered Minds*. New York: Touchstone

Kohn, Alfie (1993). *Punished By Rewards*. New York: Houghton Mifflin Company

Kohn, Alfie (1999). *The Schools Our Children Deserve*. New York: Houghton Mifflin Company

Pelzer, Dave (1995). *A Child Called It*. Deerfield Beach, FL: Health Communications, Inc.

Pelzer, Dave (1997). *The Lost Boy*. Deerfield Beach, FL: Health Communications, Inc.

Pelzer, Dave (1999). *A Man Named Dave*. New York: Dutton

Pipher, Mary, Ph.D. (1994). *Reviving Ophelia*. New York: Ballantine Books

Pollack, William Ph.D. (1998). *Real Boys*. New York: Henry Hold and Company, Inc.

Sacks, Peter (1999). *Standardized Minds*. Cambridge, MA: Perseus Publishing

The Forgotten Education

www.ingramcontent.com/pod-product-compliance
Lightning Source LLC
Chambersburg PA
CBHW072018060426
42446CB00044B/2799